THEATRE OF WONDER:

25 YEARS

# IN THE HEART OF THE BEAST

PUBLISHED IN COOPERATION WITH THE FREDERICK R. WEISMAN ART MUSEUM

**Colleen J. Sheehy, Editor**

University of Minnesota Press
*Minneapolis • London*

D1611203

Front cover art: Detail from huge parade puppet of the "Gorgeous Fever of Consciousness," designed by Beth Peterson for May Day 1995. Photograph courtesy of Gayla Ellis.

Back cover art: The Tree of Life puppet is raised at the 1991 May Day ceremony. Photograph courtesy of Salvatore Salerno.

Published by the University of Minnesota Press
111 Third Avenue South, Suite 290
Minneapolis, MN  55401-2520
http://www.upress.umn.edu


Library of Congress Cataloging-in-Publication Data

Theatre of wonder : twenty-five years In the Heart of the Beast / Colleen J. Sheehy, editor.
     p.   cm.
    "Published in cooperation with the Frederick R. Weisman Art Museum."
    Accompanies an exhibition to be held in summer 1999 at the Frederick R. Weisman Art Museum, University of Minnesota, Minneapolis.
    ISBN 0-8166-3420-3 (pb)
    1. In the Heart of the Beast Puppet and Mask Theatre—History. 2. Puppet theater—Minnesota—Minneapolis—History—20th century. I. Sheehy, Colleen Josephine. II. Frederick R. Weisman Art Museum.
PN1978.M46T44   1999
791.5'3'09776579—dc21                  99-11438

Design by Jeanne Lee and Craig Davidson

Printed in the United States of America on acid-free paper

The University of Minnesota is an equal-opportunity educator and employer.


11  10  09  08  07  06  05  04  03  02  01  00  99       10  9  8  7  6  5  4  3  2  1

# contents

# foreword

**Lyndel King**

*Director, Frederick R. Weisman Art Museum*

n 1998 the Weisman Art Museum celebrated the fifth anniversary of opening our new building, and it gives us special pleasure to recognize a milestone for another Twin Cities arts organization. We offer our congratulations to In the Heart of the Beast Puppet and Mask Theatre, which now marks the twenty-fifth anniversary of its May Day Parade and Festival.

The Weisman's exhibition *Theatre of Wonder: Twenty-five Years In the Heart of the Beast* presents the extraordinary creative work of this talented and dedicated company, which has made such a difference to the cultural life of this area. We know birthdays offer opportunities to reflect on history and accomplishments and also to consider the road into the future. That is why we are proud to present the first major retrospective and publication of the work of In the Heart of the Beast. While many Minnesotans know its work from years of outdoor May Day parades and performances at its theatre in south Minneapolis, this exhibition and book share its work with new audiences here and with audiences far beyond the Twin Cities.

In the Heart of the Beast works hard at keeping its feet— and its heart—firmly planted in its community. At the same time, it recognizes the growing international audience for puppet and mask theatre. Part of the mission of the Weisman Art Museum is to link the university and the community, and we are proud to collaborate with both In the Heart of the Beast and the University of Minnesota Press to help tell the story of this incredible community resource to the world.

*Theatre of Wonder* follows in the tradition of other theatre exhibitions the Weisman has presented in recent years. We collaborated with Minneapolis's Tyrone Guthrie Theater to present internationally renowned theatre designer Tanya Moiseiwitch, who designed the original Guthrie stage and many of the sets and costumes during its fledgling years. We organized two major theatre exhibitions and publications, *Twin City Scenic: Popular Entertainment 1895–1929* and *Theatre of the Fraternity: Staging the Ritual Space of the Scottish Rite of Freemasonry 1896–1929*, and we have worked with faculty and students from the university's Department of Theatre Arts and Dance to present special performances in conjunction with several exhibitions. So, we see our collaboration with In the Heart of the Beast as a part of a continuing effort to highlight the theatre arts as visual arts, as well as performance.

I want to acknowledge also our wonderful partners, particularly Sandy Spieler, artistic director of In the Heart of the Beast, and Todd Orjala, acquisitions editor at the University of Minnesota Press. It has been a pleasure to work with them. Colleen Sheehy, the Weisman's director of education, conceived and curated this exhibition, as well as the content of this book. It is her intelligence and creativity that are revealed here, as well as that of In the Heart of the Beast.

# acknowledgments

*From* **Colleen Sheehy**, *curator of Theatre of Wonder and director of education at the Weisman Art Museum:*

Any exhibition and book project like this one is built from the contributions of dozens of people, all of whom I deeply thank but only some of whom I can mention here. While I have admired and delighted in In the Heart of the Beast Puppet and Mask Theatre for many years, the intimate work that this project allowed has raised my high regard for its staff and work to new heights. Artistic director Sandy Spieler—dedicated visionary, remarkable sculptor, risk-taking performer, sharp thinker, amazing catalyst—has been a generous partner in this undertaking. It has been a pleasure to soak up the history of the theatre and its times in our long and frequent meetings, spanning many seasons and several years now. Similarly, Kathee Foran, executive director of In the Heart of the Beast, has helped in innumerable ways as a clear-headed leader and as an unflagging cheerleader when we needed it. During my many days at the Avalon Theater, the home of In the Heart of the Beast, all theatre staff were unfailingly cheerful and helpful in assisting with many research tasks. I especially thank Aaron Oster, Beth Peterson, Paul Robinson, Duane Tougas, and Marty Winkler.

I offer a big thanks to my colleagues at the Weisman Art Museum for contributing their consummate skills to the exhibition and for their enthusiastic support for the entire project. Director Lyndel King recognized the important opportunity this exhibition offered the Weisman, located at the University of Minnesota, to link with a vital arts organization in the community. I am grateful to her for making this project happen. I also thank Bill Anthes, a graduate student intern at the Weisman, who built the skeleton for this book's chronology through many days perusing the theatre's files. Intern Dedra Schendzielos also assisted amiably and capably on numerous behind-the-scenes research questions.

This book is a remarkable and key component of the entire project. It will preserve the theatre's work into the future and will share it with people in all parts of the nation and the world who may never have the good fortune to attend the exhibition, the May Day parades, or a main-stage production of In the Heart of the Beast. We are indebted to the University of Minnesota Press, especially Doug Armato, director; Todd Orjala, acquisitions editor; Amy Unger, production manager; Mary Keirstead, copy editor; and Jeanne Lee and Craig Davidson, designers. I also thank the writers and photographers who contributed to this volume for so vividly conveying the driving ideas, passions, and artistry of this theatre.

From **Sandy Spieler**, *artistic director of In the Heart of the Beast Puppet and Mask Theatre:*

O n behalf of the theatre, I first wish to thank Colleen Sheehy, who proposed this book and exhibition, and who with countless hours has boldly untangled our archives to articulate the wonder of this multifaceted beast. Many thanks as well to the entire staff of the Weisman Art Museum and to our editors and designers at the University of Minnesota Press for their faith in our work and their intelligent dedication to the many details involved in bringing this exhibition and book to light. Thank you for this gift in commemoration of our twenty-fifth May Day!

I wish also to extend my deepest personal thanks to the hundreds of magnificent board members, volunteers, and celebrants who have shared with their hands, hearts, and minds in shaping the artistic and organizational evolution of our theatre. A special thanks goes to those whose professional encouragement surrounded me in the fragile early years of the theatre—David and Ann O'Fallon, founders, cheerleaders, and counselors; Bryan Peterson, the spark and ringmaster of Walker Church; Martha Boesing, groundbreaking director of At the Foot of the Mountain Theatre, majestic mentor and friend; also to Jim Koplin, whose often unnamed papier-mâchéing fingers and solid critiques have assisted me as my responsibilities grew hectic. And special thanks go to my family, who patiently share me with the theatre.

My enormous respect and gratitude go now to our theatre's current staff—Kathee Foran, executive director; Beth Peterson, associate artistic director; Duane Tougas, technical director; Arthur Anderson, Alison Heimstead, Susan Hirshmugl, Masa Kawahara, Kari Kjome, Pablo, Mary Jane Mueller, Carol North, Aaron Oster, Paul Robinson, Elisha Whittington, and Marty Winkler—who not only bring this exhibition and book of past work to life, but who also hold the astute heart and brilliant energy to bring forth the next decade of wonder.

Finally, we thank Peter and Elka Schumann and the Bread and Puppet Theater, whose magnificent and soulful work ignited the first spark of inspiration for the theatre's founding, and whose persistent, generous vision and friendship feed us all.

"YOUR Community Band" heats up the street in the cold drizzle on May Day 1996. "Be a Bridge" participants, pictured from left: Robert Rumbolz, Mr. Guess, Sue Haas, Mark John, Steve Sandberg (in back), Neil Cuthbert, Steve Epp, Michael Sommers, Todd Menten, Finn Ryan, Kristin Froebel, Wendy Knox, Kevin Kling, Tom Carlson. Photograph courtesy of Salvatore Salerno.

introduction

IN THE
HEART OF
THE BEAST:
AN ART OF
TRANSFORMATION

Colleen J. Sheehy

I
n 1988, In the Heart of the Beast Puppet and Mask Theatre moved into
an old movie house—the Avalon—on Lake Street in Minneapolis that
in recent times had become a pornography theater. Soon after moving in,
the company used the building's marquee to announce in movie-
marquee letters: "Bye Bye Porn. Hello Puppets!" This act of transformation, of defiantly reclaiming a place that had become part of urban
blight, speaks loudly about the heart of In the Heart of the Beast. The
theatre's simple, true, and almost silly marquee message represents
its acts of radical transformation, of the awakening that it brought to this
stretch of Lake Street through its brilliant spectacles and soulful stories. It also
speaks of the humor and lightness of heart that dispel fear, another trademark
of this theatre company. If its heart is a place where courage, commitment,
and the saving grace of humor reside, the beast itself is the fallen and imperfect
world—Lake Street or wherever else we might find ourselves. Being in the
heart of the beast means working *there* for transformation rather than searching
for a pristine utopia somewhere else.

The transformation expressed by the porn-to-puppets sign
lies at the root of the theatre's work on many levels—material, artistic, and
spiritual. First, there is the material transformation of simple media—clay,
newspaper, paste, paint—into expressive, powerful puppets and masks.
In performance, these inanimate objects are transformed into animated figures
that engage us as real characters with that magical spark of puppet theatre.
Thematically, In the Heart of the Beast is drawn to subjects involving renewal,
rebirth, changes of heart, awakenings. Its annual May Day Parade and
Festival, which now attracts as many as thirty-five thousand winter-weary
spectators, celebrates the return of spring and the rekindling of community
spirit. Similarly, the transformation of the human heart often serves as
the subject of its main-stage productions, as in the 1993 show *Befriended by the
Enemy* based on the true story of Larry Trapp, a Grand Dragon of the Ku Klux
Klan, who renounced his Klan membership after being taken in by a Jewish
family whom he had viciously harassed. Likewise, its 1992 community pageant
*Three Circles of 500*, about the legacy of colonialism in the Americas, developed
by the company with a group of thirty community people from diverse
backgrounds, ended with a grand scene of forgiveness. In these and other
productions, In the Heart of the Beast invites us, as audience members, to face
painful truths yet also to see our lives anew as more blessed, more wondrous
than we may have realized when we walked through the doors of the Avalon.

*Theatre of Wonder: Twenty-five Years In the Heart of the Beast*
offers a retrospective examination of the work of this vital and highly regarded
theatre company in this book and in an exhibition at the Weisman Art
Museum at the University of Minnesota in summer 1999. The exhibition opens
just after the theatre's twenty-fifth May Day Parade and Festival, a tradition

launched in the company's third year; so, in fact, this project documents about twenty-seven years of the theatre's history. The story makes a stirring saga—full of passion, commitment, lively ideas, wonderfully talented and thoughtful artists, stunningly beautiful (and often funny) puppets and masks, breathtaking performances, kooky humor, and an extraordinary relationship between a theatre and its community. It also tells the tale of how a band of young artists driven to make art that made a difference evolved into a full-time company with a year-round season, a permanent home, a sizable budget, and—importantly—still driven to make art that makes a difference.

While holding special significance for those living in the Twin Cities who have worked with In the Heart of the Beast or seen its work here, the theatre's story is not bounded by Lake Street or any narrow sense of geography. During its two decades and more, the theatre's work has moved out to small midwestern towns, such as Marshall and Brainerd, Minnesota, to name just two of many. It has moved along the length of the Mississippi River, where the theatre once toured for an entire summer all the way to New Orleans. It has moved to South Dakota through stories of Anna Mae Aquash, and across the Americas in stories of Native cultures and European conquest. Its work has been seen at national puppet theatre conferences, in puppet exhibitions, and in performances abroad.

As the first major project to document and reflect on the history and artistry of In the Heart of the Beast, we know that this volume and the related exhibition will widen the theatre's circle of admirers and dedicated fans. These projects come at a time when interest in puppet theatre is enjoying a resurgence, locally and nationally. So we expect that these efforts to present in some detail the work of a theatre that has contributed in critical ways to this revival will find hungry audiences. The theatre has provided formative experiences for many theatre artists in the Twin Cities, and readers will discover woven through these pages the names of many of the Twin Cities' most innovative theatre artists, both those who have remained company members of In the Heart of the Beast and those who have gone on to form and join other companies or forge independent careers.

Like other contemporary puppet theatres, In the Heart of the Beast has reclaimed puppet and mask theatre as stirring performance for audiences of all ages. Puppet theatre in various forms, after all, has been part of human cultures for eons, and mask theatre, of course, formed the foundation of Western drama in ancient Greece. In their more formal theatrical uses, both puppets and masks have resonated with folk traditions of street performance, celebrations, and holiday practices and parades—think of Shakespeare's frequent use of masked characters at holidays and grand parties. Yet in the modern West, puppet and mask theatre became relegated to a minor status in the dramatic arts (for working classes and for children) but nonetheless remained vital in pageants, parades, and street theatre, where puppets or masked characters often could speak subversive truths or overturn social taboos. In the Heart of the Beast recognized the power of these ancient forms and the vitality of popular and folk performances, which drew it to this form of theatre in the mid-1970s. Its genius has been to forge its own distinctive art from many puppetry traditions—Japanese bunraku, Brazilian mamalengo hand puppets, rod marionettes, tabletop and toy theatres from street performance, larger-than-life three-pole puppets common to carnival and Bread and Puppet Theater, stilt-walkers from circuses and parades, and more. Through three major essays, four short literary pieces, a chronology, and many illustrations, this book aims to tell a good part of the story of the theatre's history, a complex tale involving literally hundreds of people and collaborating institutions where the theatre has done residencies over its quarter-century existence.

In the first essay, George Latshaw celebrates what the theatre has accomplished at its quarter-century mark. He holds the company in high regard. With over fifty years of experience as a puppet theatre designer and director and as a writer and editor on the subject, George Latshaw offers a broader view of the work of In the Heart of the Beast. He notes its ability to employ a variety of puppet traditions to great visual and emotional effect. In the world of puppet theatre, Latshaw observes, In the Heart of the Beast occupies a unique position because of several features: its longevity, its permanent home (rather than working as a touring company), its members' continued growth and exploration as artists, its interest in topical themes, and its ability to organize and direct a major public parade each year.

Next, David O'Fallon looks back to the theatre's passionate beginnings. O'Fallon was one of the founders of In the Heart of the Beast in 1973, along with Ray St. Louis, when they first called themselves Powderhorn Puppet Theatre. His essay conveys the political and artistic milieu of the early 1970s, when fervent beliefs and lofty aims for revolutionizing society galvanized a group of artists and activists to become puppet and mask performers and eventually form a grassroots theatre. Reflecting on the politics of the day, particularly the Vietnam War, O'Fallon conveys more immediate accounts of how ideas were translated into art and action (recalled in part from his journals from that period). Though O'Fallon left the theatre after the first several years, he and his family continued to participate in May Day parades. He has committed his professional life to promoting the arts in our daily lives, as education director of the National Endowment for the Arts and, currently, as executive director of the Perpich Minnesota Center for Art Education. His essay suggests the rich cultural life of the 1970s, when legions of grassroots arts organizations formed, many of them based on revolutionary ideas in politics and aesthetics. Some of these groups flamed and folded; many of them have grown into important arts organizations like In the Heart of the Beast (e.g., in the Twin Cities, Intermedia Arts, FORECAST Public Artworks, Women's Art Registry of Minnesota, Penumbra Theatre). Thus, O'Fallon's essay contributes to a growing historical enterprise that rewrites the simplistic and dismissive ideas about that decade.

To help readers of this volume vividly experience the work of In the Heart of the Beast, we invited four literary authors to write short pieces that would convey its aesthetic liveliness as well as its emotional and philosophical depth. Noted writers Martha Boesing, Florence Dacey, Debra Frasier, and Roy McBride have each worked closely with the theatre at different points in its history. The theme of the theatre's transformative impact echoes through their lyrical pieces.

Fittingly, positioned at the center of this book is Sandy Spieler's poetic essay on the theatre's history and philosophy. Spieler joined Powderhorn Puppet Theatre in its infancy, and as the theatre organization became more formalized, she became artistic director, a position she has held for over twenty years. With an incredible talent for creating visual poetry from puppets, movement, and music, combined with a strong sense of story, ritual, and pageantry and an unflagging commitment to community and social justice, Spieler has been the driving visionary behind the theatre. Her deeply spiritual work was influenced by her childhood as a daughter of a Lutheran minister who was involved in the civil rights movement in Washington, D.C. Yet she has also been influenced by the myths and rituals of many cultures and religions. With her enormous talents, Spieler has been able to gather around her many gifted, committed colleagues, who, as she frequently points out, have made the theatre possible. In her essay, she tells us about their philosophy of puppet theatre practice and provides great insight into the inner workings of the theatre. And she shares the saga of its artistic evolution from Powderhorn Puppet into In the Heart of the Beast, from its first, simple May Day with about one hundred people to the annual extravaganzas of recent years with thirty-five thousand participants, from outdoor performances in city parks into the multifaceted theatre company it has become today with expanded performances, summer theatre clubs for kids, and twenty residencies each year.

Both Spieler and O'Fallon mention the formative experience of working in the 1970s with Peter Schumann's Bread and Puppet Theater located in Glover, a tiny town in northern Vermont. Bread and Puppet is well known for its larger-than-life puppets used in political demonstrations and its annual summer pageant, the Domestic Resurrection Circus. While In the Heart of the Beast has definitely been influenced by Schumann's work, the company has also developed its own distinct style and subject matter by, for instance, responding to its urban setting, investigating culture and issues of the Midwest, and developing a collaborative model of artistic creation. In fact, under Spieler's direction, the theatre has explored many issues in great depth, working as a company and with many community groups. In the early 1980s, the theatre took on issues of water use and preservation, creating many pieces on the topic, including the Mississippi-bound touring show *The Circle of Water Circus* and a number of May Days. The theatre then spent several years investigating Corn—as New World plant, as sustenance, as metaphor, as contemporary agriculture—and this, in turn, led the company to devote several years to the natural and human history of the Americas before and after European conquest. The productions coming out of this topic intersected with the international observance of the 1992 Columbian quincentennial. The theatre has also shown recurring interest in Native American stories and in women's stories from the life and work of writer Meridel Le Sueur to the Italian folktale of Befana to the life and death of Native American Anna Mae Aquash. This kind of commitment to in-depth exploration of urgent themes and issues transformed into art is a distinctive feature of In the Heart of the Beast. One can trace these explorations in the detailed (yet still partial) account of the theatre's work chronicled in the time-line section of the book.

If In the Heart of the Beast takes on many of life's and history's most difficult and ponderous subjects—genocide, racism, greed, poverty of body and spirit, destruction of nature—it saves itself and its audiences from despair through its powerful artistry and its blessed sense of humor. Its work goes beyond simple agit-prop, didactic theatre to become visual spectacle and a poetry of image, music, and movement. The seriousness of its themes alternates with the zaniness of circus performances or the joyousness of a parade. Through its art and vision, In the Heart of the Beast offers us something that often seems in short supply today—the ability to reimagine the world and ourselves, to hope.

I hope that this book and related exhibition convey an inkling of the extraordinary gifts that this puppet theatre has offered to its audiences near and far. I had renewed insight about this just this past year. Having attended many May Days and main-stage productions, I was newly surprised and impressed to witness the final behind-the-scenes staff meeting before the 1998 May Day. What comes across to spectators as pure fun and revelry has a complicated checklist of "invisible" tasks (over and above the puppet and mask-making community workshops) that ensure the safety and smooth running of this major urban event—everything from parade medics to stations for lost children to final cleanup of Powderhorn Park after the all-day festival. That a theatre group of eleven full-time staff manages to do this with such grace, humor, and generosity each year surely is some kind of miracle. As Spieler notes in her essay, the May Day event is truly a labor of love, sparked by the theatre and kindled by hundreds of community collaborators. We would be lucky, indeed, to celebrate twenty-five more such May Days!

In the twenty-five-plus-year history of In the Heart of the Beast, the theatre has made its home on and around Lake Street, the border of the Phillips and Powderhorn neighborhoods in south Minneapolis. The Lake Street area has seen worse times—more poverty, more crime—and now what might be better times, with glimmers of revitalization and economic development. Through all this, In the Heart of the Beast has ministered to the surrounding community. Though Lake Street has a checkered reputation, I regard it as one of the great American streets in Minneapolis, a route rooted in history and the landscape, stretching for miles in a straight line from one major geographic landmark—the Mississippi River—to another—the shores of Lake Calhoun. It is a path carved into the earth by Native people, followed by those who settled here more recently, traversing its length on foot, on horses, in wagons, on street cars, in cars and buses, and on bikes. If we look closely, we can read the current streetscape. It tells a story of successive change, of the city moving beyond this border, of some people leaving the city on freeway overpasses, of new immigrants settling nearby, of rediscoveries of its niches and adaptable old buildings, of new building and development, of new fortunes. Despite its heavy car traffic today, Lake Street remains a great pedestrian street, lined for much of its length by small storefronts—those adaptable spaces that can easily be transformed into restaurants, clubs, record stores, shoe stores, and ethnic markets for those able and willing to take a chance and make a stand there. In this context, Lake Street and the Avalon Theater make good homes for In the Heart of the Beast.

In one of my conversations with Sandy, she mentioned that after moving to the Avalon Theater, she discovered the story of Avalon from Celtic legend. It was an island in a clear, still lake to which wounded warriors retreated for healing, where they were tended by a race of beautiful women, the keepers of courage, kindliness, and pure-hearted love. The theatre created a small puppet show of this tale and performed it for its recent capital campaign to purchase the Avalon as a permanent home. In that serendipitous and mythical way of In the Heart of the Beast, the legend truly fits.

1975

1982

1991

1990

1984

1997

Puppets for LAKE STREET MAMBO
(1990) were based on a style of Brazilian
puppets. The production used a soap-
opera style to tell stories culled
from conversations along Lake Street,
near In the Heart of the Beast Theatre.
Puppet design by Laurie Witzkowski.
Photograph courtesy of Jim Ouray.

# TWENTY-FIVE HEARTY CHEERS FOR THE BIRTHDAY BEAST

*Sparklers for Spieler and Company*

George Latshaw

**D**URING THE LAST QUARTER OF THIS CENTURY, In the Heart of the Beast Puppet and Mask Theatre has been creating visions of wonder to speak to our increasingly high-tech society. In the Heart of the Beast is definitely low-tech, or no-tech. You might even say its roots are ancient, primitive, and mystical. These Minnesota artists do not entrust their messages to floppy disks or answering machines; they go for the real stuff, human-to-human, to etch ideas on the minds and hearts of the tribe (i.e., community audience). The safest place to store ideas is in the mind site of a living being, beyond the reach of any power outage to erase what was said or acted out. The mission of In the Heart of the Beast is clearly to arouse active concern toward bettering the human condition through dramatic discourse. One of the unique characteristics of these theatre artists is the bonding partnership they have with their public, which their audience reflects back to them through loyal and loving support.

The exact history of puppetry is shrouded in uncertainty, but jointed figures, thought to be puppets, have been found in ancient tombs, and there are references to puppets in the writings of Aristotle, Horace, and Herodotus. I wrote my own "creation myth" for the opening chapter of my book *Puppetry, The Ultimate Disguise*:

> Imagine a primitive tribe reacting to thunder, lightning, fire and flood . . . to appease the furies that could bring death and destruction, there was a need to communicate—to speak and be spoken to. A name and a shape would be given to each god to bring these furies into the visible world. The shaman created the first puppets as a dwelling place for the gods, and he was both servant and master of these creations. If the gods wished to speak or move, the shaman was the "instrument" for doing it. This was not trickery, but a necessary "magic" to cope with the overwhelming fear of the unseen and the unknown. Imagine the therapeutic value of the shaman role, to be on both sides of the struggle, playing the aggressor and the aggrieved.
>
> Primitive puppets were a link between the human and the spirit worlds. . . . I believe this is the secret of the puppets' enduring service to humanity. Puppets help us to see the unseen and to know the unknown in ways that are comic or comforting according to our needs.[1]

What matters to In the Heart of the Beast is the puppet's power to evoke visions of other worlds, a power that has not diminished over the centuries. Think of our present times. We live with computers, Web sites, color television, air conditioning, minivans, jumbo jets, rocket launches, cellular phones, remote controls, fast food, Disney, designer labels—and puppets! This is one long run for the puppets, wouldn't you say? What else could be so old and look so young?

In the Heart of the Beast draws on varied international puppetry traditions for inspiration, never for imitation. The resulting hybrid is a trademark of its productions and helps to set it apart from many other puppet theatres. In the past thirty years, in fact, American puppeteers have redefined themselves as "animators of the inanimate," rather than being specialists with just one kind of puppet figure (such as marionettes). Puppeteers today have the option of controlling their figures from above, from below, from behind, or from inside. All of the puppeteer's body may be inside the figure (as in Big Bird) or only a forearm, thumb, and four fingers (as in the hand puppet). Actually, *puppet* is a family name for a whole group of moving figures. We give each one a different first name so we can tell them apart; so we have a hand puppet, shadow puppet, finger puppet, rod puppet, mouth puppet (or "muppet"), doll puppet, costume-body puppet, and string puppet. *Marionette* is used to describe only the string puppet.

The audience, once naive, has redefined itself too. Call them sophisticated or sated—never have so many been exposed to so much in so many places: entertainment in the home, the Imax, the shopping malls, the theme parks, the music concerts, the ice shows, and the circuses in three rings simultaneously. An educated public is more demanding and has come to expect the unexpected.

A field trip to see In the Heart of the Beast Puppet and Mask Theatre in performance was one of the stellar attractions of the 1994 Minneapolis Mini-Fest of The Puppeteers of America. Sandy Spieler's company was noted for choosing pithy themes. There was every reason to believe that we would encounter the unexpected, and we did! Our hosts, the Twin Cities Puppeteers Guild, shuttled us from our University of Minnesota campus meeting site to In the Heart of the Beast's home on Lake Street. It looked like a real theatre from the outside because it was a real theatre. It had a huge movie marquee above the lobby entrance, which made an imposing presence on the street. The festival delegates were abuzz to get inside to see *Befriended by the Enemy*.

## The Performance

Based on a true-life story from Lincoln, Nebraska, the first scene of *Befriended* opens with a Grand Dragon of the Ku Klux Klan trying to destroy a rabbi and his wife through vicious and incessant hate calls. The opening scene was a masterful stroke of pictorial composition, with a white-hooded hate monger sitting in a dominant, elevated position center stage, with the victims at a much lower level. It was obvious who had the upper hand. Tension and terror build and threaten to destroy the victims. When Rabbi Weisser reverses his tactics and befriends his persecutor, Larry Trapp, we discover that underneath the tormentor's hood is a pitiful wheelchair-bound diabetic who has two stubs instead of feet. It is a chilling revelation. In an extraordinary act of forgiveness, the Weissers take their former enemy into their home and care for him. Trapp renounces his former Nazi tactics and campaigns for tolerance instead, eventually converting to Judaism. He dies in the Weissers' home rather than going to a hospital.

One of the exciting features of this production was its employment of a classical Japanese puppet technique—called *bunraku*—to stage a realistic American play. In the Asian theatre it is a convention that any person wearing black on stage (prop person or puppeteer) is invisible. The black-clad handlers become "shadows," which fade into the background, and

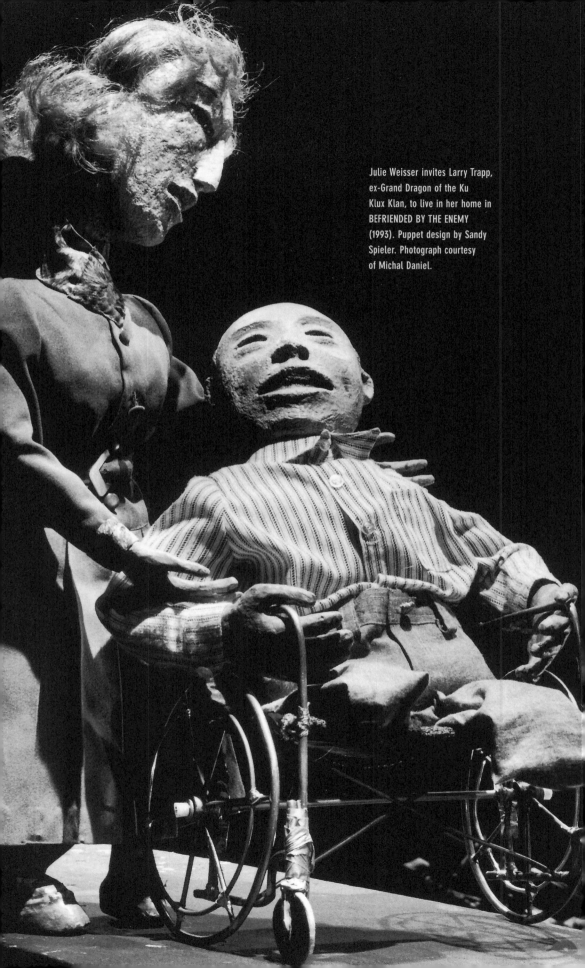

Julie Weisser invites Larry Trapp, ex-Grand Dragon of the Ku Klux Klan, to live in her home in BEFRIENDED BY THE ENEMY (1993). Puppet design by Sandy Spieler. Photograph courtesy of Michal Daniel.

the audience can focus on the puppet alone. In *Befriended by the Enemy*, this technique allowed the puppeteers to expressively manipulate the two-foot-tall puppets.

If the puppet figure used with the bunraku technique is at least two to four feet tall, the show can play to larger audiences and still be seen at the back of the house, as occurred with this In the Heart of the Beast production. The puppets perform on the same stage as the actors, above a low masking wall that establishes a ground line for the puppets and that the black-robed puppeteers stand behind. With two or three manipulators per puppet, the puppet can execute much more sophisticated moves. In the Heart of the Beast chose the bunraku-style puppets for visibility and expressiveness. They could represent real people in a theatrical way. Seeing the effective use of this style in *Befriended by the Enemy* was gratifying, for I had pioneered this Americanized bunraku style in 1958, and since then variations have become extremely popular in the United States. The bunraku-style puppets were cast in *Befriended by the Enemy* because they were the best ones for doing all the stage business in a convincing way.

In the Heart of the Beast also used larger-than-life puppets for other characters of this play, showing us another facet of its artistry. At various stages of Trapp's atonement, he is attended by angels. These magnificent beings came from behind the audience and moved down the aisles to reach the stage. Majestic in long robes with fulsome white wings, elongated necks, and African facial features painted a heavenly blue, they were a vision of extraordinary beauty, dignity, and tenderness. When they stood on stage, they almost brushed the proscenium arch above their heads, making a truly impressive sight.

## Critics' Choice

*Befriended by the Enemy* was first produced by In the Heart of the Beast in 1993 and revived in 1996. Comments by two reviewers indicate some of the impact the show had on us. Michael Tortorello, writing in *City Pages*, said:

> One of the powers of the puppet theater is that it allows artists to address prickly political issues with a playful distance unavailable in other mediums. In the Heart of the Beast Puppet and Mask Theatre . . . employ(s) a . . . metaphorical approach in this tale of a Lincoln, Nebraska Klan leader and his relationship with a cantor and his Jewish family. . . . Over the course of the first act, the cantor is first liberated from his own hatred by a weird angel, then turns his attention to converting his tormentor.

And Erin Hart wrote about the production:

> The story is told with ingenuity and humor, but as conceived by co-creators Sandy Spieler and Esther Ouray, it offers an extra ethereal dimension. At the moment of Trapp's transformation, a trio of 7-foot angels floats toward him from a deep closet full of stars. Moving slowly, with fluttering wings,

these long-necked, blue-skinned creatures cradle Trapp's small puppet body and gently pull off his white hood, transforming him with a wordless, otherworldly grace.[2]

## Afterglow from the Show

The Puppeteers of America brings together an eclectic group of people— professional puppeteers, teachers, librarians, therapists, and puppet fans—to see shows and talk shop. Some of us were moved to tears by *Befriended* and equally touched to hear the artists talk about their pilgrimage to Lincoln, Nebraska, to meet and talk to the Weissers in person. Within a year, a wire service revealed that there was interest in doing a book and a film on the Weissers, but In the Heart of the Beast had scooped them all by staging it first!

Peggy Wood, the Broadway and television actress (*I Remember Mama*, CBS-TV 1949–57), said while she was president of the American National Theatre and Academy (ANTA) that the "3 E's" of theatre were "To Entertain, To Educate, and To Exalt." There are many plays and performances that can deliver the first two, but it is a rare mountaintop to experience the third. It is the greatest gift that artists and audiences can share. In the Heart of the Beast achieved all three in *Befriended by the Enemy.*

## Larger than Life

As the angel puppets in *Befriended* demonstrate, In the Heart of the Beast makes impressive use of very large puppets. In puppet theatre, size has been one way of presenting something surprising, different, and arresting. One of the first to measure up to the task was Remo Bufano. In 1931 for a produc- tion of the opera-oratorio *Oedipus Rex* in Philadelphia, he built a group of ten-foot figures designed by the brilliant theatre artist Robert Edmond Jones. Used as visual stand-ins for the singers, the puppets appeared behind the orchestra while the singers stood to one side of the stage. The figures were operated from a platform forty feet above the stage, but they were so unwieldy that they had to be steadied by ground-level assistants with rods. For this performance, sponsored by the League of Composers, Leopold Stokowski conducted the Philadelphia Orchestra. Bufano's puppets broke new ground for musical and theatrical performances.[3]

I have had a few chances to think big and design big myself. In 1957, I received a commission from the Theatre Arts Department of the Detroit Institute of Arts to design and direct an experimental production to be performed with the Detroit Symphony Orchestra in Ford Auditorium, which seated three thousand. This challenge led me to consider a beautiful Japanese bunraku figure I had admired in the museum. It became my inspira- tion for designing the very different nine-to-eleven-foot giants to mime a Western outlaw saga to Aaron Copland's *Billy the Kid Suite.* The figures were purposely thin and flat so the audience would recognize and accept the artificial theatricality of these beings, which were floor-based and operated by two black-clad handlers each. The audience had never seen anything like this before. After the concert was over, half the audience raced toward the stage to peer down into the orchestra pit where the giants had descended to the last strains of the music. The impact was so great they did not want to leave without one last look.

Many of us have had a brush with bigness by seeing the stilt-walking clowns in the circus pre-show "walk around," or perhaps the Mardi Gras/Carnival parades came up with something tall beyond basketball. The televised views of the 1996 Olympics' opening and closing ceremonies in Atlanta showed us stilt-dancing couples and inflatable figures pumped up to the sky. Height definitely enhances the spectacle of the promenade, but do not call these figures actors.

Peter Schumann, an artist who came to the United States from Germany in 1961, is widely known today for his giant figures. He not only liberated himself from the confines of the puppet stage, but he burst out of the theatre building as well. He also liberated his audience from theatre seating and stage lighting and moved them into broad daylight and standing room only on the streets of New York. Marjorie Batchelder McPharlin, puppet theatre scholar and author, described it this way:

> Peter Schumann's Bread and Puppet Theater regularly engages in peace marches and protest demonstrations, although he asserts that it is not primarily a theatre of protest, but one in which to say things that need to be said. Theatre is a means of probing, exposing, and presenting ideas so that they get to the people. Schumann's masked actors and giant puppets, which may be eight, ten, or even eighteen feet high, have a powerful impact upon the crowds in the street, and not infrequently cause violent reactions.[4]

Schumann later moved to Vermont, where he was artist-in-residence at Goddard College for a time. He bought a farm in Glover, Vermont, where he could stage his summer Resurrection Circus on the natural hillside on his property. Preparations go on for several weeks with Schumann's "regulars" and volunteers from the community. Audiences flock from all over New England and beyond. For many it is a pilgrimage of renewal. There is a Bread and Puppet Museum in his barn, which is crammed to the rafters with the awesome images of his amazing output. Schumann has also held summer seminars at the farm for serious students.[5]

The Giant Washerwomen and Garbage Men from Bread and Puppet Theater in Glover, Vermont. They were built in the 1970s and have been used since then in shows and parades. Photograph by Ron Simon, courtesy of Bread and Puppet Theater.

Like Bread and Puppet Theater, In the Heart of the Beast Puppet and Mask Theatre also uses its voice to "say things that need to be said." Its production of *The Reapers' Tale* told the story of the arrival of Columbus in the Americas through a skeleton crew. The style was inspired by the Mexican Day of the Dead, which celebrates the departed in a festive way. The cast wore white skeletons painted on their basic blacks. Ghoulish makeup turned their heads to skulls. In the opening scene, they were choreographed in a lively line dance, until the really serious business began, depicting the foreign explorers sacking the land and killing the natives. At the end of the tale, the skeletons lay down on the floor and returned to the stillness of their graves.

The theatre's production *Table, Table*, a story about corn and agriculture, presented an eclectic mix of tabletop puppets, a humanette (a person's head atop a miniature puppet body, which is attached around the neck like a bib), hand puppets with legs (the puppeteers were visible and wore no masking sleeve to disguise the arm entering the back of the puppet), a magical, masked long-neck angel, and a shadow screen below the table, which only lit up when silhouettes were needed. The production thus used an array of puppet techniques to make a powerful point about food, sustenance, and farming.

Puppets are to poetry what humans are to prose. The way Sandy Spieler's group explore what they wish to say and how they wish to say it hearkens back to the age when the medieval guilds put on morality plays using allegorical characters to teach moral lessons. Watching a video of the Berlin Wall being tumbled in effigy during a May Day parade, I certainly sensed how the audience might have reacted to the pageant wagons of the past.

## Modern Miracle and Morality Plays in Minnesota

In the Heart of the Beast has its own ritual ground. It is a piece of theatre real estate that is not in the best part of Minneapolis, but it is home to the people who live there, and it is home to In the Heart of the Beast, who live and work there with them. Many puppeteers despair that puppets will be stuck with the "for children" label forever. Semantics have never been a problem for In the Heart of the Beast. The company knows that if you want to be considered "adult," you have to act like an adult, talk like an adult, and show adult concerns for our earth and the people in it. The key is the content that sends messages on monumental themes—the waters of the Mississippi, the farm crisis, the historic mistreatment of indigenous people—and an amazing model for defusing hate. There is nothing wrong with talking that way in front of children. They should be aware of what concerns their parents. Is that not how "heroes and sheroes" are born?

## I Love a Parade

The annual May Day parade is anticipated with glee. In a relatively short period, In the Heart of the Beast's annual theme is translated from storyboard to stunning street sight and pageant at Powderhorn Park. All volunteers are welcomed warmly. The first-timers are given guidance and work right alongside veterans who cannot wait to do it again. It is a rich intergenerational mix. There may be puppet groups in other parts of the United States who march as a unit in local parades, but In the Heart of the Beast is the only puppet company I know that designs, builds, and carries off a parade all by itself.

To prepare for May Day, the theatre is converted into a huge multipurpose room. Theatre seats are stacked against the side walls; where the audience sat now blooms with tables to become a workshop space. Other transformations also occur: external ones (on materials and supplies) and internal ones (on persons).

Creation brings personal satisfaction. A crumpled newspaper core is the base for building a face with modeling clay. The clay face is covered with torn newspaper soaked in wheat paste. The finish layer is sturdy kraft paper. When this paper ply has air dried, the clay core is removed. The result is a lightweight, sturdy shell of papier-mâché that duplicates the clay model. White paint prepares the surface for vivid colors and bold designs. Watching the progress in these stages of transformation can have a powerful effect on individuals. Allowing people to see a shape evolve that did not exist before is In the Heart of the Beast's quiet gift to the participants—a sharing of what it feels like to be an artist.

In mask-wearing societies it is thought that the spirit of the mask dwells in it, or enters the mask and empowers the wearer at the time of the ceremony. Marching and masking are good ways to escape the ordinary and explore new moves.

### The Great Outdoors

Anyone who has attempted to perform outdoors on a conventional masked marionette stage or in a traditional hand-puppet booth can describe the horrors. A gusty wind can turn the stage draperies into a sail that billows out like a hot-air balloon. You cannot allow your stage to topple over on the audience. Summer distractions abound: the birds on the wing, the passing plane, the drifting clouds, the barking dogs. The sun beating down will turn an enclosed hand-puppet booth into a sauna. When both hands are busy, perspiration will turn the nose into a water slide for glasses. The best advice is to pack up and go home before alfresco turns to el fiasco. Intimate, inside entertainment does not fare well outside.

In the Heart of the Beast can handle wide-open spaces, because its May Day shows are built to scale. The stilt walkers and the three-person pole puppets are impressive to behold. Costumes and props are designed to be seen and enjoyed at a distance. Powderhorn Park is an ideal setting for the pageant. Friends and neighbors can sit on the grassy slope and see over the heads in front of them. Powderhorn Lake provides a grand, gala entrance approach across the water by boat (or barge), which is magnificent. Even ducks gliding up off the lake add to the natural wonder of the occasion. Whatever needs to be spoken is shouted at the top of the lungs. Amplification would intrude a false note. Appreciating the difficulty for the players, the audience plays its part by being super attentive, to catch every word as it flies by.

## Home Is Where the Heart Is

The twenty-five candles on In the Heart of the Beast's cake shed light on years of work well done. In the Heart of the Beast can boast a permanent home, a season of performances in one location, a loyal following in the city, and a major Minneapolis event with the annual May Day parade. Part of In the Heart of the Beast's educational mission is to empower others with the knowledge of how to do it. Spring is the theatre's time for outreach into other parts of the state through school and community residencies. In the summer it offers teens a chance to be puppeteers in the Art Bus program, and for kids ages eight to twelve in the Powderhorn, Phillips, and Central neighborhoods, it runs a free Lake Street Theatre Club. It also has a Minnesota River Valley Theatre Club for Teachers, which offers K–12 teachers hands-on experience in creating a puppet show. These are only a few of its efforts in this direction.

For at least forty years there have been attempts to establish permanent theatres for puppets. Few have lasted for twenty-five years. Some of them include the Turnabout Theater in Los Angeles (fifteen years), Bil Baird's theatre in New York in a brownstone on Barrow Street (about ten years), Bob Baker's Marionette Theatre and party center in Los Angeles (thirty-five years), and The Puppet Show Place in Brookline, Massachusetts (twenty-five years), which the late Mary Churchill operated as a rotating venue for Boston-area and New England puppeteers. Perhaps the most expansive and well-known permanent theatre today is The Center for Puppetry Arts in the culture and museum district in midtown Atlanta, Georgia, where Vincent Anthony is executive director. It just turned twenty years old.

None of these quite fits the unique profile of the group in Minneapolis. The success and growth of puppet artists depend on the permanence of a production site and the continuity of opportunity for a creative design, performance, and production team. Sandy Spieler has provided the leadership and the spark to make it happen. Her style is lovely, lean, and spare—it is recognizably her own and like no other, but it continues to evolve and grow. The very simplicity makes it easy to embrace. No wonder Sandy and In the Heart of the Beast have found such an enthusiastic audience to support their work and cheer their efforts season after season.

## Head and Shoulders

In the Heart of the Beast has an angel or a tall, stately being figure that it uses frequently. It is a particular favorite of mine because it has a dignity and grace that come from another world. It is larger than life, of course, and looms above other elements on stage. The robes flow down from the tall, tall neck, and the arms undulate in pleasing motions. The head personifies serenity. The giant Modigliani-like creature is a tall head-and-neck mask that is worn on top of the puppeteer's head to accomplish the eerie extension. The puppeteer can see through the costume at about the chest level on the figure, which is just the place you would expect to find the all-seeing, all-feeling Heart.

## NOTES

1. George Latshaw, *Puppetry, The Ultimate Disguise* (New York: Richards Rosen Press, 1978), 16–17.

2. Michael Tortorello, "City Lights," *City Pages*, October 16, 1996, 46; Erin Hart, "Friendship Teaches Hate-monger to Hate Racism," *Star Tribune*, October 15, 1996, 2E.

3. A. R. Philpott, *A Dictionary of Puppetry* (Boston: Plays, Inc., 1969), 40.

4. Paul McPharlin, *The Puppet Theatre in America, a History, 1524 to 1948, with a Supplement, Puppets in America since 1948* by Marjorie Batchelder McPharlin (Boston: Plays, Inc., 1969), 535.

5. In late August 1998, Peter Schumann announced that he would no longer stage the annual Domestic Resurrection Circus, due, in part, to the death of a local man at the circus that year, who had been trying to break up a fight.

Angels come through the Gate of Forgiveness in BEFRIENDED BY THE ENEMY. Puppet design by Sandy Spieler. From left: Vernel Wilson, Esther Ouray, and Laurie Witzkowski. Photograph courtesy of Michal Daniel.

David O'Fallon

# IN THE HEART OF THE BEAST

*The Park, the Church, the First Show*

**A** FEW DAYS BEFORE THE FOURTH OF JULY IN 1973 some ten people carried large masks and puppet heads and poles and banners and bongo drums and the old wooden pipes from a church organ into Powderhorn Park, a few blocks south of Lake Street in Minneapolis, for our first rehearsal. We hauled our gear into the park from our aging station wagons and looked for a playing area that would provide some natural seating. There were large heads and masks, often three feet or more in length, that totally covered not only the face and head of the player-puppeteer but some of the body as well.

We built the heads in the basement of Walker Church, only a few blocks from the park. For no rent we had the use of a few tables and storage areas for supplies, chiefly hundreds of pounds of clay, boxes of newspaper, and rolls of thicker brown paper. The basic technique was simple. Masks and heads were first sculpted in clay. The clay was then covered in multiple layers of papier-mâché, ending with layers of brown paper. Then they were painted and rigged for wearing.

[OPPOSITE]
The Powderhorn
Puppet Theatre in their
second production,
FAT KITCHEN and
INTERESTING TIMES (1973).
Design by Ray St. Louis.
Theatre photograph.

To understand what brought us to this first performance, it is important to remember the bald politics of the day. Nixon was president. The war in Vietnam wore on into its ninth year. The counterculture, hippie, alternative movement had turned from a river into a thousand rivulets. Our plans (well, we did not have plans, we had visions and hopes and dreams and music) to change the world had not been put away, but their implementation seemed more distant than even one or two years before. More distant now than before Kent State, when four Ohio college students were killed by the National Guard.

In this context, Ray St. Louis and I started the theatre that became In the Heart of the Beast, born as the Powderhorn Puppet Theatre. We were burned out from years of politically directive agit-prop theatre that called for reform of the welfare system in one show and the end of the war in Vietnam in the next. Worthy goals. Wrong methods. As the scripts grew more directive and didactic, the spirit of the company wavered and dissension grew. If one is writing sermons that others must check for orthodoxy, the inevitable result is the creation of theologians, not artists. The company bickered like religious zealots. So we two left Alive and Truckin' Theatre to start something else, but what?

Then on an October night in 1972, Ray dragged his bike up the stairs to my second-floor apartment, and we looked at pictures that my wife, Ann, and I had taken a few summers earlier when we worked with Bread and Puppet Theater in Vermont. Huge figures in long white robes floated over a field. Faces as calm as the moon moved in slow procession, arms spread as wide as a street, seeming to gather up something rare and to hold it for us. Bread and Puppet sought elemental forces. It too sought to change the world but not through the overt calls to action of so many others in the theatre of this time. Rather, it sought change the way a monk might—through witness and hope and a kind of disciplined simple prayer, or practice. In the Heart of the Beast Theatre grew from seeds planted in Vermont by Bread and Puppet Theater.

Two key sites for our new theatre—Powderhorn Park and Walker Church—were poles in a political-social battery. The park had long served as a gathering place for all kinds of social and political action, energy cells of liberals, progressives, and radicals. It was possible to stir up an argument about Trotsky and democratic-centralism and picnic with the remnants of the Wobblies (Industrial Workers of the World). Walker Methodist Church, led by Pastor Brian Peterson, was the spiritual pole. To work for peace, fight for justice, speak against racism, defend the poor—for Brian this was the natural extension of the life of Christ. It was not only a matter of personal salvation that drove that church but the obligation to work toward a better neighborhood, city, world—even a better park. And these two poles—political and spiritual—were embedded in our work, in the sensibility of the theatre, as we looked at a world that troubled us more each day.

We had a president that we suspected was a crook. He was a mean-spirited man who projected his own fear-filled darkness onto the wider world. It was Nixon, recall, who labeled as "bums" the students at Kent State who later died under rifle fire from the Ohio National Guard. Nixon was much worse than a crook—he actively sought to pervert our democratic government and turn its resources, our resources, against his personal enemies, a list of people that grew longer and longer.

We thought the war in Vietnam was fought for the wrong reasons, and probably for no reasons justifiable by any ethic or moral standard. It senselessly destroyed people, their land, and their culture. We suspected that we were being lied to by the president and his generals. Our fear was that this manipulation and deceit were poisoning our culture, making it harder to act as a democracy, making it harder for people to know if their duty for a nation they loved was to stand for or against the war. We were right to think so.

In the late 1960s and early 1970s a debate was raging between those who thought the arts could directly revolutionize society and those who did not. For a few years, from 1966 or so through 1971 or '72, we thought that an enormous political, economic, and cultural shift was under way in the direction of a more cooperative and open democracy. We thought our plays and art works and songs could support and hasten a new society into reality, that art itself was a powerful antidote to lies. We believed as well that art, and theatre especially, as a public action could stir people to other public actions. We debated how art making could directly confront the abuses of power, the lies, the perversions of institutions and restore health and some balance to a turbulent, non-nourishing culture. We believed that the stakes were high. We were right. We felt that unless we did all we could to encourage a nourishing culture that we would all pay a price—a price of intolerance, of worth reduced to what one owned or controlled or had in a bank, and a growing reliance on violence.

Instead of seeing the evolution of a nourishing culture, we saw then (and now) a culture whose core value is to create meaning and personal identity through buying stuff, a materialistic consumer culture, growing faster and larger. The very images of our own minds, the content of our imaginations, were increasingly dominated by mass-produced symbols, by the messages of advertisements and the values of the marketplace.

We saw that ordinary people, the people who worked in and around Powderhorn Park, did not value their own thoughts or words or believe that they could affect the way their lives or neighborhoods worked, let alone a city or a nation. Where was the theatre that told the story of life around this neighborhood—that somehow belonged to this neighborhood?

On work tables in the Walker Church basement, cool on the hot summer days, we built up the large heads we needed for the emerging characters in the show, a sailor, a bishop, a wizard, a baker, a dragon's head, and someone called Mama. The script was a series of images, a storyboard on a sketch pad. We were building heads and masks before the story was complete. In fact, the emerging shapes began to change the story. But as we worked we fought cuteness; we trashed heads and shapes that looked as if they came directly from a cartoon, a McDonald's ad, the last Disney movie. Many did. Clay is easy to reuse. But the clay of our imagination seemed already stuck in certain forms.

Storyboard drawing by David O'Fallon for A BOAT, A BOOT, A BOOK, A BALL OF YARN (1973), the first piece performed by Powderhorn Puppet Theatre. Courtesy of David O'Fallon.

In the basement I tried to make a puppet head emblazoned with corporate and military images of the day. Logos from IBM, Coke, and Xerox, military Stars and Bars, USAP and USMC stencils, and more were affixed to it. Pieces of hardware and wires were strung about it. Great, I thought, bring all these images together. Show they are connected, that our war making and profit engines run the same car and are driven by the same fuel. I labored and added images and reworked the wires. It looked like crap, like Goofy with a phone for a mouth and hearing aids sponsored by major brands for a drag race in boot camp. I threw it out.

We were not a group of actors. We were collected largely from the neighborhood around the park. Some had experience in theatre productions in high school and college. Some had no experience at all. David, for instance, on the bongos was tracked down by Ray. One evening, as he walked through Powderhorn Park, Ray heard a complex bida bida bida boom whap bong bida. He tracked the sound to a rear balcony where a kid with wild dark hair and a glazed look was working two large bongos. A few minutes later David was part of the emerging theatre.

Our style put off traditional actors. There is something elemental, massive, and impersonal about figures that can stand two or three times human size. And when you put on a head that covers you totally, "you" disappear. You can perform for many years with In the Heart of the Beast and still have no one know who you are. For most figures there is no word, no text. The stories are narrated by one or two voices that stand outside the

action. Perhaps because of the muteness, the inclination of a head, the turning of a mask toward one is very powerful. Silence itself is a statement in a culture as noise polluted as this one. Even voiceless, the figures have distinct characters. We became agents of larger forces, the bodies and voices through which they could move.

It was not an exploration of individual histories but rather of community spaces and relationships. We needed to erect a shelter against the windchill of a savage capitalism-materialism, to carve out some space in which the mind and spirit could work. What joined us together? What connected us in the face of such mighty forces as war and greed and exploitation and the dimming of consciousness through the accumulation of stuff and things and ever more stuff?

Our puppets were large but simple, as was everything in this first show. We found or scrounged or borrowed most of what we used—scrap lumber, cloth from the homes of the company, chicken wire and staples, wooden pipes from the organ the church had dismantled. Electrical conduit from—well, from somewhere—became poles for our banners. I cannot recall how we paid for anything. There was no income. We did not charge anything. We had not applied for any grants.

Our first show, *A Boat, A Boot, A Book, A Ball of Yarn*, was performed on the Fourth of July. I paced off the distance and drove stakes for banners, making a rough semicircle at the foot of a hill in Powderhorn Park. The lake was at our backs. We drew maybe fifty or so to two shows.

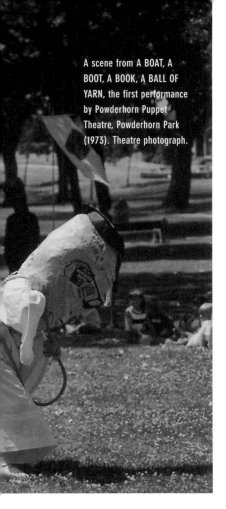

It was a simple show. I narrated a story of a people whose belief in the value and power of their own actions was symbolized by a tree on which hung the fruits of each one's work—a boat, a boot, a garment, bread from the baker, a book for the scholar. The tree is stolen from them. They struggle against the forces of state and religious institutions to get it back. But they fall into subjugation until they are awakened by a force personified in the puppet called Mama. Then they realize that their fate is, literally, in their own hands: "These hands, made each good thing that hangs upon the tree."

In an increasingly complex culture, we choose to speak as simply as possible. There is no deception here, no tricks of lighting or projections or trapdoors. The light is the day's light. The lake laps behind the show. Joggers and strollers and walkers and toddlers can be seen behind us. Some work their way along the paths toward us and stop to watch. When the tree that holds the gift of the people is destroyed by the warrior, the warrior pauses with his huge sword raised overhead, and someone rushes on, lifts the tree away, and throws down a pile of broken sticks; then the warrior completes his blow. The audience chuckles. This is childlike and delightful in that same way. Still, the tree is gone.

The show was well received. Those few dozen who saw it, including friends and relatives but also many strangers and passersby captured by the drums and the banners and then by the figures and the story, stayed and talked. We had made a modest statement on that hot summer day. We would perform the show again around the city.

Twenty-five years later it is clear that we were seed carriers and gardeners. The style of the theatre now is rooted in that first show, in simplicity, in puppets large and small and masks impressive in their mute expressiveness, in belonging to a neighborhood, a place, a community, even as the stories told have flown up and around the world, in creating a safe haven for the imagination and the spirit, in continuing the struggle to wed spiritual journey with political change.

This is a worthy struggle, and since my own life has taken me far from the theatre, I can look at it now and say with conviction how important and even essential it is. Sandy Spieler has taken a few seeds of ideas and unformed notions and created a true theatre of community. The struggle to link theatre to direct political and economic outcomes is over. We see now that we cannot move the iron monster with our songs and stories. But In the Heart of the Beast bears witness. It keeps alive a host of images and stories, of possible and potential human relationships, kept like seeds of ancient plants against the time when the monoculture comes crashing down, and we need to turn to the old fruits again, hardy in their diverse ways.

Martha Boesing

# WELCOMING THE RAIN

I AM SITTING IN A GYMNASIUM, A LARGE RECTANGULAR room with metal folding chairs and bare walls. It is an ordinary place—no magic, no illusion. There are no more than twenty-five of us waiting here. I am in the front row, and the stage in front of me has no curtain. Theatre lights are hanging helter-skelter from the beams. A small puppet theatre from the south side of Minneapolis is performing a piece called *Magnificat* here tonight. The play begins. Actors with huge papier-mâché masks move back and forth across the stage. Somehow we know that there is trouble in the land—drought and thirst. Everything about these figures looks parched. Finally a group of angry men wearing black business suits and smoking cigars stand poised around a cluster of garbage cans, which I imagine hold the debris of the mess they have made of things. They yell at each other in gibberish, interrupting one another's thoughts, declaiming their opinionated solutions to the world's problems, hashing over old scores. The earth is wounded; rain is needed—desperately—for our survival. Each one believes he holds the answer. They argue and they stomp around and they scream and denigrate each other, and finally they take off the covers of the garbage cans and bang them fiercely together, crying out for rain. But no rain comes.

All the while, a tall, thin woman dressed in simple, long blue robes, with a huge and solemnly beautiful puppet face, waits quietly and patiently, gazing out a tiny window in the back, away from all the clatter of the men. No one turns to ask her what to do. No one even notices she is there. And as she waits, tiny clouds of blue confetti—the blessed, healing rain— begin to blow in through the window, cleansing her, bathing her in goodness— as it always has, and always will.

[OPPOSITE]
**Ray St. Louis designed these puppets for MAGNIFICAT (1975), inspired by Bread and Puppet Theater's Grey Ladies. Theatre photograph.**

This is my memory of one of the first performances I ever saw of In the Heart of the Beast—or the Powderhorn Puppet Theatre—as it was called then, twenty-four years ago. It might not have happened exactly like that, but it has settled thus in my memory, etched in stone as one of the more moving theatrical experiences of my life. For a long time my own tears fell freely like the rain on the blue woman at the window, for it was I, and all of us who were there that night, who was being healed from the cantankerous noise of a society that demands that we bang on garbage containers, instead of simply stopping to notice the quiet beauty of the world we live in. And for me, In the Heart of the Beast has ever since held the promise of this image, inviting us to stand apart and trust the gentle rain.

We became compatriots in SNAC, the Southside Neighborhood Arts Coalition, a network of artists who were part of the fervent arts scene of the 1970s in the Twin Cities. We were all growing up together, coming of age—In the Heart of the Beast, At the Foot of the Mountain, Alive and Truckin', Orréa Mime Troupe, Circle of the Witch, the Palace, the Illusion Theater. There were more. We came and went. But we all saw one another's work and shared our dreams and our mailing lists and our duplicating machines and our publicity files and our opinions and our venues. At the Foot of the Mountain's first full-length play, *River Journal*, was housed in the Walker Church, where In the Heart of the Beast and the Minneapolis Ensemble Theatre (later to become the Palace) were first located.

And we shared our lights, our glue, our papier-mâché, our frustrations, our successes. When May Day first began and the parade was small, we all donned masks and brought our instruments, clay pots, and bamboo sticks and walked the route to the park, where we welcomed in the spring with the same May Day ritual that In the Heart of the Beast brings to us every year, cheering the sun across the lake, singing "You Are My Sunshine" along with the hundreds (not the thousands of today) who came to be a part of this annual ritual event. On July 4, 1976, we all climbed into Heart of the Beast's huge buffalo-head puppets in my backyard and slowly walked across the street and through the park before the fireworks began as a testimony to the great creatures of this land who have been slaughtered or caged by those of us who celebrate our freedom on this day. We were always pushing the envelope. We were rebels and we were ardent visionaries, determined to have our voices heard and to make the world a better place for everyone.

Today most of us still stand clustered in our isolation and our ignorance, banging on our garbage can lids, desperately hoping for rain—for the release from all this suffering that we have brought upon ourselves. And In the Heart of the Beast remains faithfully at the window, looking out at the healing rain falling all around us, inviting us through song and dance and magnificently beautiful giant puppets to notice how filled with blessings our lives are, if we will only take the time to see.

The Prairie, May Day parade
(1994). Puppet design by
Sandy Spieler. Photograph
courtesy of Salvatore
Salerno.

# HANDS RISING TO MEET THE WORLD

Florence Chard Dacey

**I** STILL DREAM AND WRITE IN THE HOUSE WHERE
I lived in 1980 when Heart of the Beast found me. Up in my attic,
along with versions of *Lightning* and *A Life of HOH*, letters from Sandy
Spieler, and a small, cherished cardboard star, perhaps fallen from
La Befana's magical sky, are two unmistakably Heart of the Beast four-
foot-high papier-mâché hands, somehow settled here. Rugged, blue and
open, they point toward the heavens above this small farming community.

      Reach out, with your hands, your will, your actions, your
whole body, to the world, to each other, in your particular place. That is what
Heart of the Beast is about. And blue is for the way we need to do that,
in the spirit, which is multicolored, multivoiced, multi-arted. In the 1980s, this
theatre helped me find my voices as a poet, a woman who needed her
words to be thick with passion and meaning. It showed me how to make a
mask for a dream figure, "Crazy Flo," and let her speak in a prophetic voice
about Water in a school gym in Marshall, Minnesota. In 1985 it allowed me to
honor the psychic-mythic voice that would tell the story of the first half
of my life in *Lightning*.

      Hands get messy. Heart of the Beast people pull and lift,
strain and steady, inviting us to join in this particular way to reach and touch
our imaginations, feelings, responsibilities, our communal soul. With their
very hands they make soul—images that define, deepen, and enlarge our vague
intuitions, our hazy longings, our ethical selves. We see the
Prairie, Dolphin, Tiny Dreaming Child, or the Monster
Greed, the Evil One. We murmur, gasp, or weep in
recognition. Oh, we are this, too. Together. And like
wild roses or thick slices of bread, we are gathered up,
held in hands that are music, words, paint, leaps, rage,
laughter, failure, courage, courage, courage.

      Every year, I travel 150 miles
to see this happen at the annual May Day parade. I
entreat the presences in the rivers, cedars, and herons
of my place to accompany me. In Minneapolis, we
find some of the same faces that were radiant in 1980,
high up on stilts, behind new-old masks, raising the
benevolent Tree of Life. Sandy, a steady pulse of blood
in the heart of this enterprise, is always there, resplen-
dent in her simple black dress and red hat. Smiling, she
raises the gold cymbals in her two indomitable
hands. For all of us. We are large. We gather all we
dream and know and hope might be. We begin.

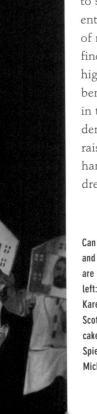

Can two be one? Rose (Elisa Randall)
and Thomas (Rainer Dornemann)
are wed in LIGHTNING (1985). From
left: wedding guests Laurie Witzkowski,
Karen Esbjornson, Kim Larsen, and
Scott Vreeland; clergy on top of
cake, David Harris. Design by Sandy
Spieler. Photograph courtesy of
Michal Daniel.

In 1990 the Minneapolis City Council approves a loan to the theatre for the purchase of the Avalon after a rousing puppet show in the council chambers. From left: Scott Vreeland, Tony Scallon, Walt Dziedzic, Marg Rozycki, and Jim Ouray (in masks). Photograph courtesy of Steve Compton.

Debra Frasier

# CAUTION—
# HEART OF THE BEAST NEAR

*You May Be Transformed*

**I**N 1996 I WAS ASKED TO TESTIFY BEFORE THE Minneapolis City Council on behalf of In the Heart of the Beast Puppet and Mask Theatre and its effort to secure funds for its building on Lake Street. It was one of the great honors of my life. Writing for this book that will celebrate In the Heart of the Beast's twenty-five years of performing comes with this profound sense of honor once again. Nothing I write will give any approximation of the wonder you feel when an In the Heart of the Beast troupe is let loose on a hillside, a street, a classroom, or a darkened theatre. But I am going to try because how often can anyone say, "I was invited to speak on behalf of something unequivocally good for the human soul"?

In order to grow into stronger people, we often borrow courage from one another, and In the Heart of the Beast has loaned our city more than its fair share. For twenty-five years this theatre has called our attention to social issues, environmental threats, and historical accounts gone wrong, consistently showing us the way to higher ground. Its members have taught us without lecturing, without didactic arguments, and without resorting to the easy dramatics of hopelessness. And after all these years, they have left us clamoring for more, even paying to be taught yet again. How have they done this?

They have done it through their astonishing sense of delight in the world and their ability to transform objects. They can make us see a hand as if for the first time, and then they can make that hand become a bird and that bird become an angel and that angel become so gigantic that her wings seem to spread out over your seat and sweep you into the show. They can even make skeletons dance in the dark of a theatre on one day and make the sun rise over a lake in a city park the next. Their courage and trust in the power of transformation are contagious. Watching them, we feel like we also can transform.

Over and over In the Heart of the Beast has made us realize that if it can do this with cardboard and fabric, we can do it with the everyday material of our lives. It helps us discover that hopes buried deeply in our hearts are, maybe—yes—they may be possible. We find ourselves saying, "Yes, yes, yes," when just yesterday we were saying, "It will cost too much." "What could I possibly do to help?" "No, not today." "YES," we nod as we walk out of the theatre.

In a world filled with opportunities to disconnect from our senses, these performances momentarily connect our eyes, our ears, our hearts, and our hands to our hopes. If people experience enough connections like these, they become everyday visionaries, making their lives creative and full of hope. Because In the Heart of the Beast is here, our city's population of everyday visionaries grows with each performance.

Last fall my nine-year-old daughter went with me to see *Web Sight*, a Heart of the Beast staging of three stories about young people who changed their small corners of the world through their work with food, violence awareness, and labor laws. My daughter came home from the theatre and immediately picked up the telephone. She organized her own food drive with her friends, collecting nearly four hundred cans in two weeks, all carried home in a small red wagon. They delivered this mound of food to the local food shelf and had their first tour of life "without." Next, my daughter wrote to President Clinton and, with shaky spelling, asked him to "do what you can" to strengthen child-labor laws around the world. (The food drive, she swears, will be an annual project. YES. The president's answer sounded a bit staged, and she questioned his resolve. She will write him again, she says. YES.)

All of this for the price of a theatre ticket! That is the kind of transformation In the Heart of the Beast has been giving us year after year. The theatre's commitment to a particular street in a particular neighborhood in a midwestern city in a farm region should not be mistaken as having less than national stature. I have seen this company transform audiences in New York City and in tiny Oregon towns. I have watched a trail of outstanding awards and reviews follow its performances, whether they be on wet grassy fields or in big city hotels with valet parking. But no matter where the theatre travels, it is never gone long, because it is a street theatre that belongs to a particular street. Our street.

In 1996 I ended my Minneapolis City Council testimony with the following:

> I worked in In the Heart of the Beast's theatre on Lake Street
> for months on end as we built [the play] *On the Day You
> Were Born*. I can tell you that they are a lighthouse on a street
> in need of light, and they have no plans to move to the
> suburbs—they understand what large thing is at stake in their
> small spot on Lake Street. This is exactly where I'd like to
> see my tax dollars spent.

And do you know, our city agreed, once again, to help support this theatre. *That* is real transformation: human beings voting dollars and cents for heart and soul. It is enough to make you proud of who we can be. Yes. Transformed, once again.

*Note: Following the many presentations on behalf of In the Heart of the Beast, the Minneapolis City Council awarded the theatre its requested federal block grant funds and went on to renew funding for renovations and acquisition the following year.*

# BEASTLY MEMORIES

Roy McBride

The buffalo created for the BUFFALO PROCESSION in Powderhorn Park on July 4, 1976. Puppet design by Sandy Spieler. Theatre photograph by Warwick Faraday Green.

## 1976

Majestic herd of buffalo

walking slow

one by one

across the Mississippi

across the bridge named

for Hennepin

circling the island

named for Nicollet

circling the waters

of our herds

ancestral memories

stirring the hearts

of the beasts.

## Priesthood of Papier-Mâché

Transformation
of space in time
off Lake Street—
upstairs from
Lake Street—
in a room
on Lake Street.

Primal stream
of life
crossing
Lake Street.

Rituals
of respect
come to
Lake Street.

Images
of everyday
transforming
Lake Street.

Chasing dreams
down Lake Street.

Around the whirl
of Lake Street.

In The Heart
Of The Beast
grows . . .

Gathering spirits.
Gathering among spirits.
Earth is holiness.
Earth is wholeness.

Sandy Spieler

# FROM THE MUD—PUPPETS
# FROM THE PULSE—SONG

*25 Years of Puppet Theatre on East Lake Street*

**W**E ARE A PUPPET AND MASK THEATRE.
As such, we are in line with an ancient and powerful
theatrical tradition whose roots lie in articulating the
mythic mysteries of human existence and the deepest
rituals of community life. This is a tradition that I
take very seriously as we build our theatre in this modern time. My mentor—
visionary poet Meridel Le Sueur—asked us as artists to "be prophets and
engineers of humanity for the common good . . . to take the image of
the people, fashion it into great forms and paeans, returning it to the people
as illumination, as love."[1]

Because our theatre was born from the political activism
of the early 1970s, interviewers often ask me if we see ourselves as a "radical"
theatre. I ask, is it radical to sing forth the vision and reality of a Beloved
Community? Then yes, I say, we are an actively radical puppet theatre. The
most radical act we have done is to consciously ground ourselves for twenty-
five years in this urban neighborhood in which we began. We have chosen to

stay in this economically troubled part of the city and to transform a former pornographic theatre into the theatre we use as our home base today. It is fair to say that our choice to be present and active during the downward cycling of our local street has threatened our survival.

Yet our survival has also been a beacon for the patient spiritual and economic revitalization of this street that we now witness. We are not a trend or an experimental fluke. We are a puppet theatre that has woven itself into the cultural fabric of this very urban south Minneapolis neighborhood, and our patient growth has been a seedbed for a blossoming of the puppetry arts in the Twin Cities.

"Our Own Stupidity" from the May Day ceremony "Voices of Trees" (1989). Photograph courtesy of Dean Hollister.

Reflecting on the vision and history of the theatre from my perspective as artistic director for two decades is a formidable task as the threads of twenty-five May Days, hundreds of performances, thousands of residencies swirl about me! The *vision* of the theatre revolves around the complex dialogue of our times and the joyful invention of puppets. The *history* of In the Heart of the Beast revolves around the many, many people who have envisioned and enacted the work of the theatre with great passionate energy. I write here of the major artistic themes from my work with the theatre, but I can offer only a peek at the thought and process that have actually involved many hands and voices.

## Wonder! Wonder?

We look at the world with an exclamation point in one eye and a big question mark in the other. Most of our work boils down to this spiritual dialectic of WONDER. Here we have been given the gift of life in a world filled with astonishing intricacies of beauty and diversity, tumultuous miracles, fomenting power, and the patient relentless cycle of birth, death, and birth again. The expression of this wonder leads us to advertise what it is that makes life worth living! It has us enacting great pageants that joyously revel in the obvious yet mysterious connection of all things. Still in the midst of this glory, we witness the awful poverty of body and soul perpetrated by the hatred of self, "the other," and the earth. This foreboding wonder calls us to untangle the artificial constructs of racism, classism, sexism, and inexplicable greed. It asks us to dance down the linear fear of death that manufactures systems of excess and genocide—and ultimate defeat. Our exclamations and questions spiral according to the internal and external pulse of the times, giving rise to the specific content of our work over these years.

We are a puppet theatre because the pure metaphor inherent in this ancient tradition clearly expresses the soulful act of transformation that words cannot speak. As we lift an object to life on the stage, we enact the

The Tree of Life is lifted by the Newman family group of ten puppeteers, 1980. Theatre photograph.

mystery of our own birth. As we lay the object back in its resting place, we experience a certain death. As a puppet walks, it is a conduit for the energy that rises from the ground to fill the beat of our own hearts. We are a constant witness to this most amazing transformation, and it expresses the larger intrigue of the creating, destroying, and healing powers of nature, and the human hand, heart, and mind. The act of transformation is the essential core of puppet and mask theatre. And it is from this dynamic center that we work.

As puppeteers we inherit a powerful ritual legacy rising from the earliest expressions of one's connection to each other, to life and death itself, to a spirit world. The first puppeteers were shamans and street wanderers. In many ways our work is more closely aligned with this ancient shamanistic theatre than with the more narrative structure of Western European theatre. All our pageants and many of our shows are structured according to a ritual progression of actions. Our work emphasizes the physical, emotional, and spiritual relationships between the players, and we build our "dialogue" with musical and movement narratives as well as words. Primary characters may be crows, rivers, infants, and cities as well as men and women. Heroines may travel through landscapes of time, battle inner demons, or wrestle societal monsters of great proportions. Clowns often speak at moments of great seriousness. With this poetic form of theatre we express the many layers of waking and dream life that revolve around us each day. We invite our audience to respond with their deep emotions as well as their minds (and their good senses of humor!).

Each show begins with some essential core of an idea. We almost never begin with a formal script, but rather with the raw tools of our work: idea, image, gesture, puppet, word, music. Sometimes early ideas demand research involving anything from live interviews, trips to the library, journeys to other regions, images from dreams, or group discussions. Though there are common techniques and skills we all use to develop new work, each artist creates in his or her own unique way. I am always surrounded by image flashes that move between my thinking head and my dreaming heart. When I have gathered my early ideas, I call my coworkers together with sticks, cardboard boxes, cloth, tape, and odd assortments of instruments to "brainstorm in action" according to the working threads of the core images.

Kevin Kling demonstrates his early idea for the "funny fish" during rehearsals for THE CIRCLE OF WATER CIRCUS on the farm in Alma, Wisconsin. From left: Mark John, Steve Epp, Mari Olafsdotter, Sue Haas, Kevin Kling, Doug Cain, and Esther Ouray. Theatre photograph.

This is always a feast day for me! It is a treasured privilege to behold the pure genius of my colleagues as they create with raw purity and kookiness. Here, everyone thinks in motion, everyone contributes ideas. From the spin of the fabric, the click of the tongue, the odd gait of a box moved across the floor, I catch the poetic glimpses from which I plan the puppet design and draw a structured storyboard. This storyboard then becomes my map for the layering of puppets, sound, words, light, and paint.

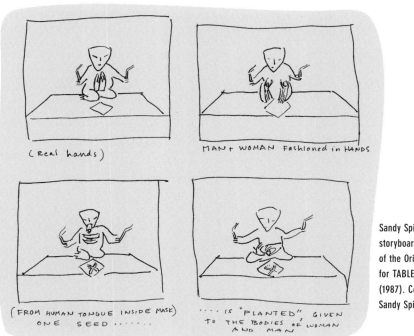

(Real hands)

MAN + WOMAN Fashioned in HANDS

(FROM HUMAN TONGUE INSIDE MASK)
ONE SEED ......

...... IS "PLANTED" GIVEN
TO THE BODIES OF WOMAN
AND MAN

Sandy Spieler's early storyboard sketch of the Origin Shrine for TABLE, TABLE (1987). Courtesy of Sandy Spieler.

Our puppets are often inspired by the rich world traditions of puppet types; yet each is invented uniquely for the current production. Each puppet is designed for movement. Each is sculpted for a certain iconographic expression. Each is rehearsed to find its own peculiar gesture. We often build our puppets from supplies at hand and frequently recycle the wonderful junk found in alley dumpsters into various parts of puppets and sets. Many of the puppet heads are sculpted from cardboard or clay and then layered with papier-mâché. This is a lengthy process and a time when many volunteers enter our workshop to help. As the front-page headlines and comic pages of local newspapers are torn and layered into place for the skin of our puppets, so are the stories of the many people who work on the puppets. The energy of all this flies about the stage or the street as these puppets are lifted to life and baptized by the audience response.

Throughout the year we now enact many different types of puppet work—main-stage shows for adults, main-stage shows for families, one-person shows, cabarets, touring shows, ritual events, residencies, proces-sions, and the annual May Day Parade and Festival. Years ago the theatre functioned with a certain tribal osmosis—everyone did everything necessary to produce and enact the work. As the years have progressed, a more delineated system has emerged in the organizational structure, with separate artistic and administrative teams that work very hard to produce full-time wages and support such a broad spectrum of work. As artistic director, I am at the hub of many decisions, but not all. Since the mid-1980s many different artists have initiated main-stage work, and all company members share various leadership roles in the creation of our work.

There are endless ways to direct the creation of new work. In puppet theatre, the visual language of the piece is intrinsically important, structuring the narrative in a similar way as a script might work in non-puppet theatres. Thus, the functions of conceptualizer, designer, and director are difficult to separate, and in fact are often carried by one person. When working with a collaborative team of creators, the team must "meld into one mind" and operate with a great deal of trust, especially between designer and director. Sometimes we have used a more collective process intended to include a large group not only in the performance but in the writing and building as well. In such instances, we have put work on stage created by novice participants side by side with the work of our veteran puppeteers.

Our residency work in schools, colleges, churches, and community organizations in cities and small towns most often uses puppetry for the discovery and articulation of the participants' own ideas and puppets. Here we work as midwives, teaching puppet techniques but also teaching the participants how to form their stories from the body of their own community. Whole neighborhoods come together for the enactment of such local pageants.

## In the Heart of the Beast

Perhaps it seems like a contradiction to be a professional theatre with a community soul. Our internal dilemmas—about speaking our artistic voices while also giving community participants a voice; about providing our company with livable wages while keeping the theatre work inexpensive and affordable—are not separate from the external dilemmas of the larger world. Indeed, such a path contains all the recurring dilemmas of seeking to live a soulful life in the midst of our nation, where everything is valued primarily as a commodity of the marketplace. Walking this dilemma is part of being "in the heart of the beast."

In 1979, company member and poet Steven Linsner suggested the name "In the Heart of the Beast" as a metaphor for our theatre. He wrote,

To be puppeteers in the Heart of the Beast

. . . is to find ourselves in the great world Beast made of families, races, ages, sexes, classes, corporations and nations, people, (and creatures!) all different, working out a way to live together.

. . . is to work puppets. To hold life in our hands, to sense how we are all like puppets—worked by instincts, voices, and forces above us and below us.

. . . is to carry and protect something very old like a heart within us, a secret, a promise. Like carrying a flickering candle through a dark place. Like carrying a family in a horse-drawn wagon.

. . . is to travel the roads of history and loss, in search of
something like a new heart: new communities, new families,
new work, new holidays.

. . . is to tell the story of people who live in the heart of the
beast—as courageous and resourceful as they really are.

All words and philosophies aside, the true memory of twenty-five years is the
one lived by the hundreds of people who have raised the theatre with their
hands, hearts, and minds. The puppeteers, musicians, managers, and volunteers
who have walked together through all the jolly times and all the dilemmas
with passionate energy, enormous faith, and consummate skill. The conver-
gence of all participants has produced a lengthy and lively trail of work, which
we have attempted to retrieve for the timeline in this book. Here, I recount
only the evolution of some of our major artistic themes within my experience
with the theatre. My wish, however, is for all my colleagues to be remembered
and honored for their contributions to the organic development of the theatre
we are today. A true history would take a great book, written from the tongues
of many—artists and administrators alike.

## Basement Beginnings, Befana, Buffalo

As a child, I was happiest when I was sculpting. Faces mostly. Out of anything
I could find. Soap or plaster or snow. I was raised in a minister's family in
Washington, D.C., in the midst of the Vietnam War protests and great marches
for civil rights. When I went to college, I intended to be a doctor but came
to Minneapolis in 1973, seeking a way to reconcile my spiritual ethics with the
political horrors that were happening nationally. I landed in the Almond Tree
Household, across the street from Little Earth of United Tribes, a community
of new housing for Native Americans in the Phillips neighborhood. As a
collective, our household actively participated in the life of the Phillips
neighborhood—one of the poorest in the Twin Cities—and organized regular
celebrations for the purpose of "bringing people together." Still intending
to be a doctor, I started working in the local hospital, and somehow I ended up
sculpting again. Heavy, life-size plaster figures. A friend who had studied at
Goddard College in Vermont remarked that my figures reminded her of the
Bread and Puppet Theater. She knew of the fledgling Powderhorn Puppet
Theatre in the basement of Walker Church only six blocks away, and advised
me to "check it out."

      The Puppet Theatre was about seven months old at the time
and was offering puppet-making classes in their corner of the basement. The
workshop was small—two tables, two buckets for all the clay, and one set
of shelves for all the tools and storage. Still, this basement was in the hubbub
of all the activity in this church, which had become a center of experimental
theatre and political activism. The Puppet Theatre had just received a neighborhood revitalization grant to bring small puppet shows to day-care centers,
parks, and senior centers. I applied for the job and was soon performing with
a team of three others: Ray St. Louis, the director, a solid showman with
underplayed wit and considerable puppet skill; Ric Watson, a mask-movement
wizard; and Polly Harvat, a talented gem just out of high school.

With a larger group who had been part of the theatre shows in the previous year, we planned our first indoor "pageant" for the stage at Walker Church, *The Grass Will Grow and the River Flow*. The title was taken from the treaties that had been made between the U.S. government and Native leaders with the promise that they would not be broken as long as "the grass will grow and the river flow." We opened with the presentation of huge puppets of Earth, Water, the Seasons, Fire, and Wind. Bursting into this natural world was a Faustian circus of Devils, Boy Scouts, Faust himself, and a hand puppet Master of Ceremonies. Their antics were foolish as they degraded each other and bargained with their destructive ambitions. Into the wasteland they created, I remember playing my first mask—a Bird Woman who fed the birds with the simple faith that the birds would come and that seed would fall to the earth again and again.

That winter of 1974, I suggested the Italian story of *La Befana* as our small show to bring to all the community sites and holiday parties of our touring circuit. *La Befana* is the legend of the old "witch" who travels around the world for one thousand years looking for the Holy Child, only to discover that *"All children are holy,"* that the illumination of love is carried inside each of us. I realized how this legend must have risen to carry an important thread of feminine wisdom from the ancient earth religions into the patriarchal Christian church that was marching across Old Europe. Polly Harvat played the masked figure of Befana. Eileen McCormack was the narrator, who also played the toy piano. Ray St. Louis and I performed all the other puppets. We used mostly hand puppets and rod puppets worked above a simple curtain to animate Befana's journey around the world.

La Befana (rod puppet) begins her journey around the world. From the small touring version of 1981. Theatre photograph.

Little did I realize then that *La Befana* would become a classic of our repertoire, with twelve versions repeated over the years. It evolved from its simple beginnings into a six-person

Anna Mae is shot! From the tabletop show about Anna Mae Aquash, May Day, circa 1982. FROM LEFT: Steve Epp, Sandy Spieler, and Marg Rozycki. Photograph courtesy of John Franzen.

touring show and then into a main-stage production, using twelve puppeteers and musicians, plus youth interns and child performers.

Befana's journey creates a lens through which we examine the current state of children and the elderly in our culture, and has given rise over the years to some scenes of great pathos (such as the year a ten-year-old was shot down the block) but also of great comic satire (such as the year "the baby prince" William of England was born). As a main-stage classic, the old crone Befana is still performed by two actors—one wearing a mask, the other speaking her voice as a narrator/musician by the side of the stage. Befana's journey is now a feast of puppet magic, as she is sometimes a very tiny puppet, sometimes very large. With the turn of a piece of cardboard, we create entire landscapes—a desert, a forest, a crowded slum, a palace. A suitcase contains a winter's blizzard. The figures of a nativity crèche become huge looming figures to calm a nightmarish dream. And Befana's journey always culminates with her exclamation for the whole world to hear, "*All children are holy!*"

The year 1976 was the U.S. bicentennial, and I was obsessed with the disparity between the voices of Native Americans and the history taught by the Founding Fathers of the United States. I listened to my neighbors at Little Earth of the United Tribes and heard the powerful speeches given by the leaders of the American Indian Movement. One week after May Day that year—on Mother's Day—the story of Anna Mae Aquash arrived on my doorstep in the morning newspaper. Here was a Native woman who had worked in the Twin Cities, teaching children and gathering oral stories from her elders. She had also been involved with the American Indian Movement encampment at Wounded Knee. The newspaper said that she had been found dead in a South Dakota field and that the FBI took her body and buried her away from her people. Her family exhumed her body and found that she had been shot point-blank in the back of her head and that her hands had been cut off and sent to Washington, D.C., for fingerprints. Anna Mae's story tore across my heart. At that moment I knew I would consecrate the work of my hands to building stories that would speak against such atrocities. I would speak with my puppets in all the ways I could imagine to coax out the qualities of human goodness that can prevail over such horrors, building new paths for us to walk on.

I visited Powderhorn Park quite frequently in those days. There seemed to be a pulse rising from this site of the ancient Sun Dance, and I thought of the buffalo who walked over this ground before the United States was even a notion in anyone's head. And I remembered the horrible story of the buffalo being shot to near extinction a mere hundred years ago and about the larger metaphor of this destruction, the despicable treatment of the American Indian people at the hands of our Founding Fathers. I saw women walking across the grasses of the desecrated prairie, following the buffalo, who thundered over the ground. And I kept seeing the large sculpture of Abraham Lincoln, sitting in his chair, overlooking the great marches for peace and freedom that poured into Washington, D.C. I saw millions of people standing there under this huge figure, speaking their visions and their pleas for justice in this land, and Lincoln with his head in his hands, weeping.

And so we created a herd of huge Buffalo puppets and gathered in Martha Boesing's backyard, across from the park, on the "official" bicentennial—July 4, 1976. Together with women from At the Foot of the Mountain Theatre and numerous other volunteers, we donned the Buffalo and began walking. We walked down the hill and circled through the entire park. We walked in silence except for the single strain of a mournful banjo. The Women of the Dust followed the Buffalo, and after them came the great puppet figure of Abraham Lincoln, sitting in his chair upon a wheeled cart; he had his head in his hands, weeping. Finally, there was a group of children dressed in yellow and pulling a red wagon that carried a little tree covered with yellow birds. The children danced their birds with such clarity and joy in their faces, a certain prayer for renewal. And I knew—all of us knew—that we had enacted a powerful rite on that day.

Later that year we brought the Buffalo to New Orleans and then to Washington, D.C., to join thousands for the Continental Walk for Disarmament and Social Justice on the steps of the Lincoln Memorial, the very site that had so inspired a key image in the Buffalo Procession. Anna Mae, too, continued to follow me. The following year (1977), I performed a lament for Anna Mae as part of our May Day ceremony (*The White Show*) with a choir of thirteen women. Several years later, I built a very simple table-top show of Anna Mae's story, which we have performed for numerous events in support of Natives' rights.

The years we spent in the basement of Walker Church were a vital seedbed for much of our continuing work. Here we built many puppets for a number of popular shows—*Magnificat*, three versions of *The Prairie Circus*, two versions of *The Christmas Story*, four versions of *La*

*Befana*. These years were also filled with the wrestlings of a passionate young group of theatre artists. There were power struggles, moments of brilliance, and plenty of ideas that, in hindsight, were just bad. Ray St. Louis left the theatre in 1976, and I was appointed "temporary" artistic director by our advisory board. We were then a group of ten or so, who were the mainstays of the theatre's work. All of us were balancing our work at the small theatre with the work we were doing to support ourselves. Some of us wanted to make puppet theatre our life's work, and others wanted to work only time to time on the shows demanding more participants. We had clearly outgrown our corner in the basement. Steven Linsner, Margo McCreary, Curt Sloan, and I defined ourselves as a guild, determined to make an ongoing organization while sharing the directorship of new shows.

In 1979 we changed our name. We were performing and teaching out of town quite often, and our audiences asked us why we had taken the name *Powderhorn*, which is actually a military term, and so we decided to change our name. We changed it officially on Valentine's Day, announcing it with an impromptu performance. We quickly made some simple puppets with just white sheets and sticks that would actually stand up in the waist-high snow to enact a simple Valentine's poem that Steven Linsner had written about our name change. We hopped into the back of a pickup truck that night, stopped at several vacant lots around town, and jumped into the snow with our puppets to simulate Wind, a Spider, and a Man with a Fiddle. The finale featured a big White Monster that spewed forth a dancer with a Heart mask, dressed totally in red, twirling torches of Fire. Probably a total of one hundred people saw this completely unannounced piece of guerrilla theatre telling of our new name: In the Heart of the Beast Puppet and Mask Theatre. This name was inspired by a phrase written by the Cuban poet José Marti, though often attributed to Ché Guevara. Ché had urged North Americans who wanted to be part of the Cuban revolution to "stay home and work in the place where you live, where you find your community, in the heart of the beast." We wanted to tell stories from the center of where we lived, from the center where the heart beats, the place of change. The next year, with this new name, we moved to a storefront on East Lake Street in the Gustavus Adolphus building.

## May Day

The spring of 1975 was our first May Day Festival. The original impetus was quite simple. We wanted to give a gift to the community that was supporting us and to create a celebration that would bring people together out of their houses at the end of winter. More important, the day was a "holy" day for important roots of our theatre's sensibilities—the "green root" and the "red root." The green root is the ancient Nordic earth calendar root, marking the time when spring blossoms in all her glory. The red root is the blood root, the people's labor root, originating from the 1886 Chicago garment workers' strike and growing into a worldwide celebration of labor solidarity.

During our initial May Day planning, the Vietnam War was still raging, and we planned our parade as an event of community rejuvenation in the face of this national tragedy. Happily, the war ended just weeks before the event, and our little procession was exuberantly joyful. It was a group of fifty or sixty people, an Earth puppet, a Water puppet, several birds, accordions, and many banners. We reached the park and raised a puppet maypole; there were a few small performances and some political speeches, and everyone got sunburned; then we went home. It poured rain that night.

In 1976, the second May Day happened with a stronger idea about the ritual quality of the event. We began to see the procession as an important transformational act of moving from one place to another. We developed a small performance for the beginning of the parade and for the end as we raised the maypole. Our planning group from the year before had been divided by an ideological split within the local food cooperative movement. This "Co-op War" had split marriages and households as well as organizations, with passionate disagreements and even some violence. We chose the theme of Noah's Ark for the parade, as a metaphor for traveling through this storm. Feelings were riding high, and we were frightened that the May Day parade might be stopped. We were not.

We were stopped the next year, in 1977, by a group of protesters who thought we had stolen May Day from labor. I stepped forward and stated that our intention was to enact this procession as a way to celebrate the workers who build this community every day with the creativity of their hands, hearts, and minds. And we continued on with the procession. By its third year, our May Day parade had become a tradition that could not easily be broken.

Twenty-five years later, the organizing work of the festival is a year-round task. In February we host our first public brainstorming sessions, when we invite all to share ideas and images to devise the specific theme for the year. The thoughtful themes of the past years echo the pulse of our south Minneapolis neighborhoods, and as such, the chronology of themes tells a peculiarly imaginative history of the times. To develop the theme, the May Day staff take ideas from the public meetings and research them, dissect them, argue them, and finally name a theme. Then we craft a simple Parade Story and draw it out on a storyboard as a series of images. The story is divided into specific parade sections, each designed musically and visually by the staff artists who serve as the directors for the puppet, mask, movement, and musical creations of their section.

When we open the doors for the public workshops during the first week of April, hundreds and hundreds of people of all ages pour in to work according to the storyboard, either building their own creations or helping with the larger parade puppets. At first sight, the public workshops seem like a chaotic hive of buzzing bees. On closer inspection, one can see the parade story emerging from dizzily busy hands molding clay, stapling fabric, and laying paint. I consider these public workshops to be the heart of May Day, for it is here that neighbors of all ages meet each other in new ways. And it is here that I witness imagination flourishing like dandelions. The parade is built by many, many hands with a unified energy that is quite contagious.

On May Day, the parade explodes onto the street, blessing this artery of communication and commerce in a new way. We tell our theme story section by section, proceeding down the street like a walking Burma-Shave sign. We own the street for the day, playing instruments that usually sit at home in the corner, strutting masks with fiery verve. We welcome back the spring birds and greet neighbors from near and far.

One of the May Day workshops in the Avalon Theater, 1996. Theatre photograph by Warwick Faraday Green.

The parade culminates with the Tree of Life Ceremony in Powderhorn Park, enacted on the shores of Powderhorn Lake, where a natural hillside amphitheater serves as our performance space. The event has evolved from a simple maypole dance on the first May Day to our current tradition, which involves hundreds of performers. The ceremony takes its inspiration from the theme for the parade. Yet it also holds the larger ritual that is central to the day itself, tying directly into the green and red roots of May Day. The pageant always enacts the foibles of the "Everyday People" and their courageous dealings with the various inflictions on the human spirit, our community spirit, and our earth spirit. We ritually welcome the return of the sun to our part of the world as we paddle a huge Sun puppet across the lake, resulting in the momentous rising of the Tree of Life.

Our huge puppets representing the Woods, River, Sky, and Prairie usually open the ceremony and remind us that we humans always act within the context of the broader community of animals, plants, the elements, and time. The "Everyday People" are often the only unmasked players of the ceremony and function somewhat like the ancient Greek chorus, as instigators of action and "focus-ers" of the larger picture. They always represent the best vision we humans can muster from our perspective in this time and place, often coming to grips with their own destructive tendencies.

May Day's brilliance is grounded in the consistent generous gathering of a group of artists, neighbors, and organizers whose thinking and skills have evolved with the festival itself. The pageant usually involves about two hundred participants, necessitating a rather simple but grand plan. I have directed the ceremony each year, and the entire May Day staff brainstorm with me for its content and actions and then become section leaders for the big public rehearsals. Steve Sandberg has been musical director all but one year (when Robert Rumbolz directed). Michael Sommers and Mick Labriola have been important percussive cue masters of the action; Jim Ouray and Nanci Olesen, the narrators/ringmasters on stilts. Since 1977, the Newman family group has been "Keepers of the Tree of Life," organizing a group of friends to tend, repair, rehearse, and perform this important puppet. The responsibility for orchestrating the Sun Crossing has been handed down year by year to many leaders: Connie Harris, Bruce Blacher, Loren Kellen, and Jekke Shaten. Over the years we have also been graced by guest artists from around the world who have come to live with us in the months leading up to May Day. Each participant has added to the inventions and techniques of our "cardboard art" and to the flair of the ceremony.

Having started on a small patch of land on the shore of Powderhorn Lake with a few dozen people, our ceremony has now burst the seams of its natural boundaries of trees, shore, and hill as, in recent years, some thirty-five thousand people watch, cheer, boo, clap, and sing. Someone described it as a cross between a circus, a grand historical pageant, and an ancient ritual. I simply see it as an intense act of love, an invitation to return yearly to a feast of community, joy, and renewal.

## Lake Street, the Farm, the Water Years

In the summer of 1980, I attended the Union Internationale de la Marionnette (UNIMA) conference in Washington, D.C., and returned with renewed vigor to build soulful work growing out of the stories and aesthetics of the Midwest, which I saw as a missing link in an otherwise inspired conference. And then, that same summer, I led a puppet workshop at another conference. For this one we camped on the edge of the windswept prairie, in the foothills of South Dakota's Black Hills. This conference, called the International Survival Gathering, was led by Native visionaries, who spoke late into the night with astute, searing speeches about the global economy with its distressful social and ecological impacts. We gathered at this spot to protest the uranium mining in the sacred Native land of the Black Hills, which the federal government had ordered for the growing nuclear power industry. We were told that the mining operations would totally deplete the already scarce water table.

As I listened to the passionate orations about the preciousness of water, I thought of a book recently sent to me by a Japanese friend, called *Give Me Water*. This book of memories from Hiroshima and Nagasaki portrayed the horrified victims of the nuclear blast running to the river with their bodies on fire, screaming, "Give me water!" Instantly I understood the deep cyclical way water moves through our lives physically and spiritually. I had the idea for an epic pageant that would travel the lifeline of the Mississippi River with the vision of this circle of water. Serendipitously, at the Survival Gathering, I also met Jim Ouray; he and Esther Ouray would become major partners in what would become known as the Water Years at the theatre.

With direct inspiration from the Survival Gathering and the anxious tide ushered in with the Reagan administration, we created a new show for Christmas in our tiny storefront space. I wanted to present the essence of the biblical Christmas story with its generous revolutionary prophecy of love in a modern local context. I thought of the Holy Child being born in a garage hidden and protected by "Underground People." These were the people keeping their culture intact despite living in a neighborhood that was abandoned by the fancy city economy and disdained by the righteously sentimental and dangerous King Herod (Reagan). I called this show *The Hunt*. We built a stage that suggested a prairie landscape, with an inner box that functioned as a toy theatre stage. A great blue heron, transformed into the angel Gabriel, the Underground People, and the Holy Family were crudely fashioned rod marionettes. The City People were played by knives, forks, and spoons. King Herod was a slick ventriloquistic dummy. The Ancestor Angels were tiny, floating primitive masks of prairie animals, reminding me of the voices speaking into the night with that South Dakota wind.

Somehow this production marked a new era for the theatre. The Ourays, newly arrived from Florida, and Marg Rozycki helped to build and perform *The Hunt*. Soon after, Steve Epp, Nanci Olesen, and Karen Esbjornson came from the tutelage of David Olson of the Cherry Creek Theatre in St. Peter, Minnesota. We started in earnest to plan three years of water shows and residencies to culminate with an extended tour on the Mississippi River. We hired Lucinda Anderson as the only paid staff to help us carry out this plan administratively.

As we developed our ideas, we laughed that each show we would build about water would begin with the phrase, "Once . . . the world . . . was a great . . . sea." And so began our first water show, *Oh! River!* in 1981. This was a fable of two brothers, one a "Lover," the other a "User" of water, and in between them, the River herself—ancient, seductive, essential, and

The Moon loves the River from OH! RIVER! (1981). Rod puppets designed by Sandy Spieler. Photograph courtesy of Bob Olsgard.

untamable. The brothers were awkward life-size rod puppets. The river was a graceful rod puppet, fluidly changing faces, and at times transforming into the huge enveloping cloth of the sea that filled the entire stage. The six of us in the cast created a vocal sonic design, with some dissonant, improvised structures and some haunting, lyrical melodies.

We brought the theme of water into our out-of-town residency work as well, and working with such a wide variety of people helped us articulate images that would repeat in later water shows. A particularly seminal production was held in Marshall, Minnesota, in 1981. It was here that we met poet Florence Dacey, who wrote these deceptively simple lines about the circle of water:

> When we forget the water, we forget the child who begins in
> the water
> When we forget the child, we forget ourselves
> And then,
> We forget the world.

In the summer of 1981, we built the four great puppets we now call "The Big Ones"—the River, the Woods, the Sky, and the Prairie—when we were asked to create the opening ceremony for "The Gathering," a national theatre conference sponsored by Cherry Creek Theatre in St. Peter, Minnesota. Basing our work on Meridel Le Sueur's poem "Let the Bird of Earth Fly," we inaugurated The Gathering with four processions: the River on a raft floating on the Minnesota River, the Woods from the north, the Prairie from the west, and the Sky, a great eagle, coming from the east. Meeting in the center of town, we enacted a brief ceremony, and then with the shouting of Meridel's great poem, we released the "Bird of Earth," with all the energy of dozens of hands sculpted on its large face.

We were now gathering people who would become the company for the Mississippi River Tour, and together we began work on a major indoor epic, *A Life of HOH*, to speak to the way water intertwines our spiritual and physical health. *A Life of HOH* was brainstormed by the entire company of thirteen, using a storytelling process I had learned while studying Balinese mask theatre. We began with the question, "Your mother will die unless she can have a drink from the Water of Life. Where do you go and what do you find?" We repeated our stories again and again, changing and combining details each time the story was told.

We then invented three siblings—Hardin, Olivia, and Henry (get it? H$_2$O!)—who journey through all the different landscapes of physical and metaphysical water that pervade our lives. Hardin, the oldest, looks to "the experts" for the solution, but the lack of available answers leads him to desperate actions, jail, and a descent into the Sewer World, which brings him into his own Desert, joined by Parched Animals. Olivia, the second child, follows the River to its northern source. She finds the frozen world that binds all emotions. She rescues a Child from its cage of frozen tears, meets the women who bend to the Water, then follows the River through the cycles of life and death back to the Ocean. Henry, the youngest, follows the water pipes to the comical pumphouse of the city and eventually to the frightful future of the Underground Aquifer, where water is a measure of wealth and power. He meets the Little Green Man, who gives him a dried seed. Henry's tears make the seed grow into a common apple. With the unique music of hose horns, vocal collages, and the "water cello," these journeys twisted around each other to a bitter yet exultant finish. Created by a fantastically skilled and inventive company of puppeteers, actors, writers, and musicians, *A Life of HOH* was a popular success.

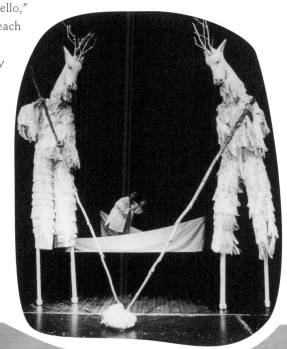

From A LIFE OF HOH (1983): The Snow Deer (Steve Epp and Nanci Olesen) find the baby wrapped in its cage of ice. Olivia (Esther Ouray) prepares to rescue the child. Puppet design by Sandy Spieler. Photograph courtesy of Bob Olsgard.

The River enters St. Peter, Minnesota, on the Minnesota River for the opening ceremony of The Gathering, a national theatre festival, 1981. Puppet design by Sandy Spieler. Theatre photograph.

Now all our attention turned toward the production of one more May Day (with "Water" as the theme of course), and then—with twenty-five adults, five children, and two dogs—we headed to the Gust-Winje farm in Alma, Wisconsin, near the Mississippi River to create *The Circle of Water Circus*. We spent two months on the farm, living and eating together, filling barn and field with the inventing of puppets, music, and epic circus scenes. Opening our show in July in Brainerd, Minnesota, near the headwaters of the Mississippi, we traveled the river for four months, ending in New Orleans on Halloween weekend. We bought a school bus and a houseboat, which we took turns riding on, and laughingly called our boat the *Collapso*, satirizing ocean explorer Jacques Cousteau's boat, *Calypso*, which was on the Mississippi that same summer. The *Collapso* did indeed collapse—it simply died and would not go any farther and was put on the docks a little south of St. Louis. We continued on with our school bus, camping by the river each night, or staying in homes or church basements, watching the river turn from a tiny brook into the ocean.

We tried to be at each stop of our tour for a couple of days. Over these days, we would work with the local people to build puppets and masks related to a specific aspect of the river in that town's history. Then we would enact a River Parade, which would lead to the site of the circus performance. We first performed Side Shows, created by teams of two to four company members, about different aspects of water. Then, the Big Ring Show told "the story of the Mississippi River from the Ice Age to the present moment," but it also enacted the essential and universal story of the preciousness of all water.

The Big Ring Show began with a prologue of the River's birth out of the Age of Ice, and a Presentation of the River's Natural Life of Fish, Snake, Turtle, Alligators, Black Birds, Bear, Buffalo, and finally the Early People. The unfolding grandeur of this pageant was slashed by the abrupt entrance of Hernando de Soto, which brought a change of mood and style, shifting the performance into a progression of historical scenes presented as circus acts. Thomas Jefferson and Napoleon waltzed with the giant River puppet as they bargained for the Louisiana Purchase, ushering in a scene about "Manifest Destiny" and the resultant tragic Trail of Tears for the Native population. The fancy Mississippi Steamboats pranced about like white horses. The first bridge was made from Acrobats. The Civil War was fought by identical armies, and Madame Hemoglobin's Trained Mosquitoes towered over the audience on stilts of various heights. With the propelling beat of the Circus Band, the birth of the blues rose from the River Delta, and the Moon and River danced their eternal romance.

[OPPOSITE]
Madame Hemoglobin's trained mosquitoes! Watch out! From THE CIRCLE OF WATER CIRCUS (1983). Pictured in height from small to large: Finn Ryan, Nick Wroblewski, Kevin Kling, Nanci Olesen, Jim Ouray, and Steve Epp. The River puppet looks on. Photograph by Kent Kreigshauser, courtesy of the MACOMB JOURNAL.

Interspersed throughout were the clownish acts of the Everyday People, who demonstrated our everyday use of water with great veracity until they were hypnotized by the allure of the Poison family. They changed the face of the River to the Mask of Poison, resulting in sickness for all. Our cast of children entered the scene and played simple bells to wake the adults who lay poisoned in their self-destruction. They ritualistically

uncovered the face of poison from the great River Puppet, as we shouted Meridel Le Sueur's poetic plea for purification. We carried in the huge puppets of Woods, Sky, and Prairie to join the River in reminding us once again of the basic sustenance of our lives, whose future health lay in all of our hands.

*The Circle of Water Circus* changed the theatre forever. News of our theatre spread throughout the country. People started to come to work with us from faraway places. We were asked back to the towns along the river for residencies, to help other artists start their own companies, to build parades and performances. On the invitation of an international theatre festival, we took the circus to Sweden and Denmark in 1985. The group of veteran performers who worked and lived so intensely together have remained puppeteers and theatre workers in many important venues in the Twin Cities, and year after year they return to In the Heart of the Beast with their consummate skill and energy to help the work of May Day and other projects happen. The bond from six months on the river is deep.

## The Third Floor and Corn

We paid for the circus by the extravagant gift of artists working for ten dollars a week plus food and sleeping-bag lodging. We returned to Minneapolis with a debt from the broken-down *Collapso* and a storefront space we had entirely outgrown. Most of the circus group picked up their lives where they had left off, and the core that remained at the theatre produced a seventh version of *La Befana* and the tenth May Day. After many discussions about the possibilities of moving permanently to a farm, we decided to stay in our urban neighborhood. Sometime in the summer of 1984, we moved our workshops nearby to the third floor above Roberts Shoes at the corner of Chicago Avenue and Lake Street. Our years at Roberts Shoes were marked by a variety of shows with a variety of directors and newly invented puppet forms. Despite our penniless conditions, we made a firm commitment to begin paying a full-time staff to produce shows and conduct an expanded residency program.

One of the first productions that we created in our new space was a new version of *The Hunt*. Connecting it to the growing concerns with political oppression in Central America, we told the story of Mary and Joseph knocking on doors, seeking asylum from King Herod's army, as a metaphor for the refugees who were escaping the violence of their countries. Our old workshop space at Walker Church had recently been turned into a sanctuary to house first a woman and then also a man from Guatemala as part of the growing sanctuary movement among U.S. churches to harbor refugees from El Salvador and Guatemala. We made the puppets from flat cardboard to create a kinetic mural effect on stage, inspired by the grand storytelling painting of Mexican artist Diego Rivera.

Then we produced something entirely different—an operatic love story, *Lightning*, performed at the Southern Theatre in Minneapolis. Unlike most of our other work, this was a collaboration between artists, not a company working improvisationally together. Opinions varied widely as to its success. One critic called it "astounding . . . it was a remarkable visual pageant of symbols, scenes and colors . . . as startling and illuminating as a bolt of natural lighting." Another said it "belonged in a museum with Elvis Presley paintings."[2]

Michael Sommers and Loren Niemi created an actor and puppet version of *Beowulf*, which Michael likes to call "a noble failure." In 1985, Michael curated our first Experimental Studio Series, which gave local puppet artists an important venue to present new ideas in form and content. The beginning of these series marked the significant growth of puppetry as a vital form of adult theatre—a contagious effect of having an ongoing established puppet venue such as In the Heart of the Beast.

Martha Boesing and I cocreated an adult version of Hans Christian Andersen's fairy tale *The Nightingale* in our intimate sixty-seat theatre. Because Martha had worked primarily with actors (rather than puppeteers), I designed the piece for actors whose movement would be informed by the sculpted gestures of puppet theatre. We worked with the actors to hold even their facial expressions in a masklike way, changing a bit from emotion to emotion. The fairy tale is about the certain death that happens when a culture forgets its soul. In the story the soul is represented by the Nightingale—first a real bird, simple and wild, who is then replaced by a jeweled, golden music box bird. Esther Ouray played the wild bird, her almost naked body painted all blue, and we used a mannequin, gilded and mechanized, as the fake bird.

Continuing the plan to use our small Roberts Shoes space for performances, George Sand, Jim Spieler, and Michael Sommers created a children's matinee called *Odd, I See*. This zany journey of a child lost in the city featured fun visual trickery as well as a film sequence.

At about the same time, many of us were continuing the thread of our interest in Central America, and we found ourselves discussing "Corn" as a metaphor for our ancient agrarian roots, connecting North, Central, and South Americas. We began research for a series of shows based on the idea of corn, and found Meridel Le Sueur's epic prose poem "The Origins of Corn," which gave us a vibrant, dense text that outlined much of our early thought. Corn became the theme for May Day that year (1986), and we filled the streets with figures of Tigers, Suns, Corn Planters and Eaters, and many forms of Corn itself. We dedicated this parade to Meridel Le Sueur, then eighty-six, as a way to honor her considerable influence on our theatre's vision.

Writer Meridel Le Sueur participates as a special guest in the May Day parade, circa 1985. Photograph courtesy of Ann Luce.

The Corn theme led us into conversations with farmers and people involved with land stewardship and agriculture policies. Jim Ouray directed a piece to take to the schools about farm issues and the rural-urban connection. *The Story of Corn* featured a wonderful puppet of a young girl named Suzie (played by Kitty Kuluvar), whose fascinating look into the history of corn begins with her bowl of cornflakes one morning. With the great musical team of Mark John and Barb Cohen, the story moved throughout the ancient Mayan and Aztec worlds to the modern farmers of the American Midwest today. *The Story of Corn* also focused on the economic systems that control most of the food production today. Jim led some residencies in rural communities based on the large issues of farm and land policies.

Influenced by the deepening economic plight of small farmers at the time and the resulting rash of farmer suicides, I began work on *Table, Table*, which was based directly on Meridel's poem. The piece was virtually wordless, developed through a series of narrative images and abstract vocal sounds invented by Steve Sandberg. We built a series of animated Corn Shrines, which framed small parts of the puppeteers' bodies (mouth, eyes, hands, tongue). Each shrine personified a particular historical period. The Origin Shrine presented a single kernel of corn from its tongue to the man and woman who formed in its hands. The Hungry Pyramid consumed reams of miniature peasant figures, grimacing with its distorted latex mask. A decorated Corn Palace (inspired by the Corn Palace in Mitchell, South Dakota) sang for the festival of corn. The imposing Chicago Grain Market framed an eerie head that ate money. One very funny scene employed a host of toylike wooden puppets to enact the corny Corn Parade. The end of the piece was a haunting "Resurrection of the Seed Corn." After the suicide of the Farmer, the Farm Wife began the act of planting, winding into a furor that raised the memory of all the people who have planted for countless ages, rising as corn, growing in multitudes.

During *Table, Table* the fire marshal declared that we could no longer use our third-floor space for public performances, so we knew it was time to move once again.

### The Avalon and the Quincentennial

In 1987, Lucinda Anderson led the search for a new space. Just up Lake Street at Fifteenth Avenue, the Avalon Theater sat empty, having recently closed as a pornographic movie house. Lucinda successfully lobbied for us to move into the building and secure funds for its renovation. The space was a wreck when we moved in, but Partner's Three Company tackled the management of many volunteer squads and of many professional contractors to scrub, paint, and bring the building up to code.

That first year in the Avalon, our puppet work exploded with joy in this raw expansive new space. In the fall, as yet without chairs or stage, we staged a wacky Experimental Series—a Halloween-inspired labyrinth of performances called *House of Mysteries*—then launched into our tenth version of *La Befana*, the first main-stage show at the Avalon. *La Befana* was followed by the very popular *The Invisible Child*, cocreated by Jeanni Calvit, Mari Olafsdotter, and a guest artist from Czechoslovakia, Rostia Cerny. Rostia was an expert in the form of "black light" theatre, a popular puppet form that creates the illusion of objects floating through space with puppeteers in total "invisible" darkness. This technique was the perfect way to tell the story of a young girl who chooses to be invisible until she is loved back to visibility by a family of oversized trolls. Both *La Befana* and *Invisible Child* performed to sold-out audiences in our huge new space. That next spring when we opened our doors for the fifteenth May Day Parade Public Workshops and unexpectedly ended up hosting hundreds of people, we realized the sudden leap of public support that surrounded our move to the Avalon.

Many of us continued working with the Pan-American themes that were begun with *The Story of Corn* and *Table, Table*. Laurie Witzkowski had joined a peace walk (Marcha por La Paz) in Nicaragua and called us with the realization that our work was connecting with the much larger quincentennial movement that was stirring up all across the Americas. The upcoming 1992 observance of the anniversary of Columbus's arrival in the Americas was raising all the issues of what it means to be a multicultural nation. Whose voice is it that defines our culture? How do we address—and change—the legacies of colonialism? For several years, from 1989 through 1992, we investigated these issues in our main-stage shows, May Day festivals, and other work.

When Laurie returned home, we started work on a series of quincentennial events and thought it fitting to begin with a savagely ironic look at the story of Christopher Columbus himself. This first quincentennial show opened in the fall of 1989 with the official title *The Reapers' Tale: A Celebration in the House of the Dead, Featuring the Grand Feast of the Skeletons and Their Reenactment of the Great Voyage of Christopher Columbus in Honor of the Life of the World*. Laurie, Martha Boesing, and I cocreated this piece with the gathered company. Performing in October, we stylized everything according to the Día de los Muertos (The Day of the Dead), where all of the characters (and sets) were skeletons—King Ferdinand and Queen Isabella, the Soldiers, the Native People, Columbus and his Ships, even the Wind. The audience sat along both sides of the theatre. On one end we built the Cathedral of the Old World, decked out with skeleton gargoyles, and on the other end was the Shrine of the New World, complete with ten-foot statues representing Earth, Wind, Fire, and Water. In between was the Great Ocean, which worked both metaphorically and literally to examine the great distance between the two worlds.

All the performers began on the floor as skeletons sleeping in their graves while the audience entered. They rose from their graves to enact the journey of Christopher Columbus to the New World, his first encounters with the Taino Indians, and the continuing acts of genocide perpetuated by the later conquistadors. In the heat of a great *danse macabre*, a fifteen-foot skeleton Conquistador toppled the head of the central shrine, sending red sand gushing out of the statue's mouth, like the incalculable volumes of blood spilled on the land. Then began the portrayal of the modern vestiges of the Conquistadors. A TV set, a huge Car Tire, Shopping Malls, and Corporate Skyscrapers all rolled down our sloping theatre floor, crashing into the stage where the New World had been desecrated. Finally, two full barrels of Coke cans clattered onto the floor. The huge Puppet of Darkness entered and reached down to pull the fragile globe from the rubbish and placed it gently into the arms of the Old Woman. The skeleton performers began the Prayer for the Life of the World (from the poem by Latin American writer Eduardo Galeano), each speaking in a different language: "When greed comes to an end, the face of the world will be set free; its hands will be set free, its feet will be set free."[3] Then all the skeletons returned to their graves.

The Reapers' Tale surely opened the quincentennial issues for us, but because we were primarily a "white" company, we created a midwifing committee composed of many different cultural voices to continue the dialogue. This group discussed the central ideas for all the projects that would unfold, culminating with the quincentennial year of 1992. The next project was to develop a piece for families and schools. Laurie, Roy McBride, and Beth Peterson created Discover America to teach about the cultures of the Americas before the European invasions. They heralded the Salamander who first stepped onto the dry land as "the real discoverer of America." They explored the inventions and philosophies of Native cultures from the four directions. They introduced early explorers from Africa, Asia, and Europe, and finally, in the last five minutes, Christopher Columbus arrived with a rapid explosion of railroads, churches, town, and cities. The finale introduced us to four children from our own time who sang about each of their own culture's contributions to the United States, ending with Roy McBride's catchy rap refrain "Who Discovered America?"

Meanwhile Dhann Polnau and Paul Chamberlain built Anaconda, with an exceptionally beautiful stage filled with three-dimensional papier-mâché trees through which emerged all manner of plant, insect, and animal life to explore the life of the Amazonian Rain Forest before the coming of the Conquistador. The company spent time moving in the mud flats of a river delta to replicate the writhing, sensual world of the deep forest for their performance of Lantern Fish, Red-Faced Monkeys, Alligators, the Panther, Live Snakes, and huge puppets of Rain and Spider. In the final scene, an imposing Anaconda snake puppet (jointed for remarkable movement and spanning the width of the entire stage) wrapped itself completely around the human Conquistador. The Anaconda then slyly climbed back into the trees, peering into the audience with its brilliant red eyes.

To remember and honor the enormous contributions of the Native peoples to the Americas, we chose the theme "Return to Turtle Island" for the seventeenth May Day celebration in 1991. That was the only year in our history when the parade and the ceremony were both rained out. The day arrived, and it poured and poured and poured. And poured. And then the rain turned into snow. We were huddled in the theatre with all of the parade puppets and the many people who had come from out of town who could not stay until the postponed date the following Sunday. Among them were two Native elders, Floyd Westerman and Clyde Bellecourt, who laughed together. "Of course it rained today!" they said, "Turtles bring rain!" So the joke was on us!

We used the 1991 Experimental Series as a way to offer artists of many different cultural perspectives a venue to express their views of the legacy of the Conquistadors. Here I met Dong Il Lee, a director from Korea, who led the audience through a shamanistic masked dance ritual to "purge our houses" of the colonialist spirit. Dong Il's roots in both ritual theatre and political street theatre surrounded our work in 1992, the year of the actual quincentennial.

In observance of the quincentennial, we chose the Mayan phrase "I Am Another Yourself" as the theme for the 1992 May Day. We thought it spoke clearly for the need for us all, particularly in this year, to remember our connection to the web of all creation. Two weeks before the day of May Day, Rodney King was brutally beaten by police in Los Angeles, resulting in riots across the nation. Tensions were high in Minneapolis, too, and we considered different ways to express a way of dealing with such racial brutality. We finally came back to our chosen theme for the day. In the ceremony, we portrayed a tense "stand-off" between "the Everyday People" and some big figures representing institutionalized greed and its violent sidekicks. The audience wondered if this would turn into a theatricalized battle with one side or the other winning out. Instead, the Everyday People stood still, across the field, each purposefully raising a letter that boldly spelled out "I AM ANOTHER YOURSELF." The Family of Greed paused a moment, and, awkwardly at first but then equally purposefully, they lifted off their masks and stepped out of their puppets to reveal themselves simply as "another yourself." Idealistic or naive, you might think? Perhaps. But our purpose on May Day is to put forth the most positive vision we can muster, boldly risking that our imaginations manifest themselves in the real true action of our everyday lives.

We then turned our energies to the creation and production of the final piece of the three-year-long quincentennial series, a complex community pageant, *Three Circles of 500*. The piece was to portray three circles of time: the first, the five hundred years before Columbus; the second, the five hundred years from Columbus to the present time; and the third, the five hundred years from now into the future. The core cast was thirty, the whole cast one hundred. Most of the assembled group was new to the theatre and new to the art of puppet theatre. I codirected this piece with Dong Il Lee, and we all purely wanted this piece to be written and built by everyone. There were many heated discussions and some actual physical fights, the issues ran so deep. We found many places of common humanity on which we could agree, but as to the details of the story, we discovered that the truth was that no one could ever agree on any one point of view, that history differed enormously depending on one's personal experience. In exasperation the day before we opened, we finally decided to scrap a particular scene and in its place to give each performer twenty seconds to do or say whatever their heart so dictated. This was, of course, the fitting way to mark the many voices of the Americas that we are. The event was framed by a larger ritual that dealt with the external forces of the Conquistador but also challenged the ways we each carry the Conquistador mentality within our everyday lives.

In researching this piece, I listened to so many personal stories of incredible pain that I wondered how large my heart would have to grow to find a place for so much sadness. One of the Native elders in our community talked about the genocide of her people, children being taken off to school, her family killed, the terrible problems with alcohol. After years of searching for a way to reconcile the details of her life, she talked about putting on the "shawl of forgiveness," and with this, she said, she knew she could survive. So we made eighty of these shawls and put them on near the end of the pageant to enact a passionate dance with spirit hoops. The hoops were then passed to each person of the audience, and they were invited to tie their visions for community healing onto the hoop with a piece of cloth. Indeed, this was a theatre piece with rough edges, but many in the community thanked us for this timely ritual.

The mid-1990s brought a distinct change on our section of Lake Street. Drugs, prostitution, and a rising homicide rate brought us again to look at issues of community wellness. Our quincentennial events presented the themes of "undoing racism," in broad, epic pageants. The next years led us to celebrate the creative actions of neighbors figuring out a way to solve these epic issues in their own lives. *Befriended by the Enemy* was based on a true-life story of courageous forgiveness between a Jewish family and a Nazi Klansman. Esther Ouray and I traveled twice to Lincoln, Nebraska, to develop our piece from live interviews. The touring show *Our Place*, a direct sequel to *Discover America*, was also assembled from interviews and life stories, and directed by Laurie Witzkowski. The creative team (Beth Peterson, Andrew Kim, Roy McBride, Julie Kastigar, and Elisha Whittington) conducted workshops with fifth-graders from a local school to weave the tale of four neighborhood children finding a way through their family problems to build supportive friendships with one another.

## A Lake Street Theatre

We have continued work at the Avalon with various people in the company, initiating new work. Big shows, tiny shows, ritual events, cabarets, installations, singing shows, and residencies continue to emerge from the buckets of clay and piles of cardboard always ready in our workshop. The stories and songs continue to rise from the hands and hearts of my numerous coworkers, the diligent "engineers of the imagination."[4]

In 1991, Roy McBride and Beth Peterson initiated the Lake Street Theatre Club in response to the many neighborhood children who began "hanging out" at the theatre, and it has continued each summer since then. This free summer camp is specifically for the youth from the three neighborhoods immediately surrounding the theatre. The young people create the content, the puppets, and masks for several short stories and learn other performance skills such as drumming and stilt dancing. We also began hiring local teenagers to work with the younger children as intern-mentors. By 1996, the teens had also begun creating their own touring show to perform for block-club parties, summer schools, and park centers each summer, traveling via "the Art Bus," a lively painted van. With guidance from Heart of the Beast artists, the teens develop their own shows based on their life experiences and soaring imaginations. Some of the children have now "graduated" to the teen program, thus creating a viable peer mentoring process.

Art Bus 1998. Cast members of "Baby Camp," the humorous story of how one teenage girl makes the decision that she is not yet ready to have a baby. FROM LEFT: Tamara Jackson, Louise Kegg, Francis Cloutier, Asia McSwain, Termaine Finley. Masks by Art Bus students. Photograph courtesy of Gayla Ellis.

Native Elders from THREE CIRCLES OF 500 (1992) (designed by Chris Warren and Eva Two Crow) with cast members (from left) Andrew Kim, Julie Kastigar, Laurie Witzkowski, Anna Stanley, and Eva Two Crow. Photograph courtesy of Dayton's.

Thus, by the mid-1990s, we were fully grounded as Lake Street artists with the Avalon as our home base and with much of the operating structure by which we function today. And how did we emerge from the basement corner of Walker Church into a full-time company with possession of an old movie theatre as our permanent home? That is a complex story in itself, but thanks is largely due to the lineage of resourceful, hardworking, and very dedicated administrative teams and boards of directors. Our administrative directors—Lucinda Anderson, then Wilma Wernick, then Nadya Ruebenova, and now Kathee Foran—led us through the complicated negotiations to purchase the Avalon Theater (finally successful in 1998), and bit by bit established year-round wages for our full-time staff. Our full-time artistic staff of eight possess many diverse skills, including the talents of an "official" technical director, a need that became more and more apparent with our move to the Avalon, and was filled first by Mark John, then Greg Carter, and now Duane Tougas. Our outreach programs grew and grew with the visioning and tending of an outreach director—first Roy McBride and now Beth Peterson as associate artistic director.

We now produce our work in a yearly cycle: in half of the year we build and perform our main-stage productions, and in the other half we work within the broader community doing residencies, May Day, and Lake Street Theatre Club. In this way we also divide the use of our building. Half of the year it is set up as a performing space, and for the other half, we stack away all the theatre seats and open the space as an active building

workshop. Thousands of people pour into this building on East Lake Street to partake in the investigation of wonder from in the heart of the beast.

Our impetus has not really changed from that first fable enacted in Powderhorn Park in 1973, and our establishment of a permanent home and support for a full-time staff has happened gradually, according to the organic growth of the company. Our work and our company continue to evolve with inventive chutzpah as we wrestle with the current conundrums of the times. It has been my unique privilege to have walked these twenty-five years with colleagues so full of vigorous vision, skill, and love.

Now, I am still happiest when I am sculpting. And as I stand on the threshold of the new millennium, I think once again of the image of the Tree of Life, which is each of us and all of us. Twenty-five years ago, I built the giant Tree of Life puppet and with quiet intuition rose it up in the center of our May Day celebration. There is a pulse of something ancient that asks to speak through this puppet. An invitation to join in this great feast of life where all are relatives and where there is plenty to share. An invitation to live in the splendor of life's adventure, always changing, always growing, falling, and then rising again. As I watch this Tree rise up year after year, it takes on more power, filling me once again with the awe of this Beloved Community, and I am reminded that twenty-five years is a very brief moment indeed. Just a blink.

## NOTES

1. Excerpt from an unidentified book, published by the Federal Writer's Project in the 1930s, encouraging women to be writers. From clipping file of Meridel Le Sueur, given to Sandy Spieler.

2. Madeline Douglas, "Lightning," *Vinyl*, April 15, 1985; C. L. Thrale, "Better Luck Next Time," *Twin Cities Reader*, April 10, 1985.

3. Eduardo Galeano, *Memory of Fire*, trans. Cedric Belfrage (New York: Pantheon, 1967).

4. Phrase inspired by the book *Engineers of the Imagination: The Welfare State Handbook*, ed. Tony Coult and Baz Kershaw (London: Methuen, 1983; reprinted, 1990).

The Tree of Life (masked version) shares one of the generous "ordinary gifts" with the "ordinary person and her family" (Silvia Maria Zuñiga and community participants) from the beginning of the May Day ceremony in 1990. Theatre photograph.

# IN THE
# HEART OF
# THE BEAST

*color plates*

The buffalo created for the
**BUFFALO PROCESSION** *in*
*Powderhorn Park on July 4,*
*1976. Puppet design by Sandy*
*Spieler. Theatre photograph*
*by Warwick Faraday Green.*

Flower bearers, May Day 1977. Purple-faced women masks worn by women from At the Foot of the Mountain Theatre. Design by Sandy Spieler. Photograph courtesy of Warren Hansen.

*In* SHOES OF INFANT LIGHT
*(1981), Uncle Harold (Steve
Epp) is kidnapped, bound, and
tossed into the Belly of Fear.*
Pictured: *Karen Esbjornson.
Puppet design by Sandy
Spieler. Photograph courtesy
of John Franzen.*

The Italian townspeople, over-
sized masks from LA BEFANA
(1991). Design by Sandy
Spieler. From right: Laurie
Witzkowski, Maria Roon,
Roy McBride, and Greg
Carter. Theatre photograph.

[OPPOSITE]
La Befana (Lisa Belfiori)
invites the Magi (Greg Carter
and Pete Angilello) into her
little house. Puppet design
by Sandy Spieler. Theatre
photograph.

# A LIFE OF
# HOH

WATER STORY #3
IN THE HEART OF THE BEAST THEATRE
JAN. 20 – FEB. 13
EVERY THURS.– SUN., 8:00 P.M. GROUP RATES AVAILABLE
WALKER COMMUNITY CHURCH    3104 16TH AV S.
(CALL H.O.B.T FOR TICKETS 724-9302)    MINNEAPOLIS

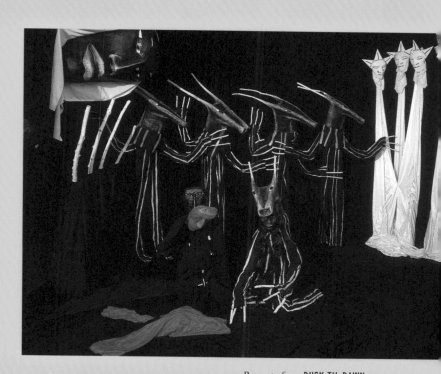

*Puppets from* DUSK TIL DAWN
*(1984). From left: the Dark
Maiden, who transformed into
a skeleton; the Night Beasts;
the Man in Red sheds his skin;
and the Stars. Puppet design
by Sandy Spieler. Photograph
courtesy of Gerald Gustafson.*

[OPPOSITE]

*Poster from* A LIFE OF HOH
*(1983). Design by
Sandy Spieler. Courtesy
of Sandy Spieler.*

*Mary, Joseph, and their dog as seven-inch-tall rod marionettes from the first production of* **THE HUNT** *(1980).*

*Abbie, Peggy, and the Silent One, the Star Seekers in* **THE HUNT** *(1980).*

*The Underground People from* **THE HUNT** *(1980). Puppet design by Sandy Spieler. Theatre photographs by Warwick Faraday Green.*

Oversized, flat cardboard puppets from the second
production of THE HUNT (1984). Puppet design by Sandy
Spieler. Photograph courtesy of Gerald Gustafson.

The Angel Gabriel (Andrew Kim) visits Mary (Esther Ouray) and her dog
(Alison Heimstead) in the field of corn (Debra Ramos, Aaron Oster) in
the Annunciation scene from THE HUNT (1997). Puppet design by Sandy Spieler.
Photograph courtesy of Michal Daniel.

*"Spinning the Blood Thread"*
*dream sequence from* LIGHTNING
*(1985).* Pictured dancer:
*Elisa Randall.* Puppets: *Karen*
*Esbjornson, Mary Benefiel,*
*Donna Roberts, and Laurie*
*Witzkowski. Puppet design by*
*Sandy Spieler. Photograph*
*courtesy of John Franzen.*

In **TABLE, TABLE,** *a piece of corn is presented from the tongue of the mask wearer to the figures in its hand (1987). Designed and performed by Sandy Spieler. Theatre photograph by Warwick Faraday Green.*

*"Thought and Flesh of the Americas." Corn bodies designed for* **TABLE, TABLE** *by Sandy Spieler (1987). Theatre photographs by Warwick Faraday Green.*

*Chief Seattle with words
from his famous speech
woven around him. From the
thirteenth May Day, "We
May Be Family After All,"
1987. Puppet design by Jim
Ouray. Theatre photograph.*

*Lord Pooh (George Sand)*
*presents the gilded "bird" to the*
*Emperor (Pauline Pflandler)*
*and his court (Maj Britt*
*Specktor and Holly Schwartz)*
*from* **THE NIGHTINGALE** *(1986).*
*Puppet design by Sandy*
*Spieler. Photograph courtesy*
*of Doug Pipan.*

The Emperor (Andrew Kim)
hears the nightingale's song
(Elisha Whittington) for the first
time in THE MOST BEAUTIFUL
THING IN MY KINGDOM. Designed
by Sandy Spieler for the
Experimental Studio Series,
1998. Theatre photograph by
Warwick Faraday Green.

*Christopher Columbus (Laurie Witzkowski) captures an Arawak woman (Esther Ouray) from the Shrine of the New World in* THE REAPERS' TALE *(1989). Puppet design by Sandy Spieler. Photograph courtesy of Salvatore Salerno.*

*Christopher Columbus (Laurie Witzkowski) kneels before Queen Isabella and King Ferdinand of Spain before he sets out on his voyage to America. From* THE REAPERS' TALE *(1989). Puppet design by Sandy Spieler; skeleton cathedral design by Jim Ouray. Photograph courtesy of Salvatore Salerno.*

*Poster for* **THE REAPERS'**
**TALE** *(1989). Design by*
*Sandy Spieler. Courtesy of*
*Sandy Spieler.*

*From* ODD, I SEE *(1986), Cornelius with Grandma's eye, which follows him everywhere. Puppet design by Jim Spieler. Theatre photograph.*

*The dollar tempts Eugene Hassenfus as he sits in his easy chair. Using a recent story from the newspaper, Jim Ouray designed and performed this piece in 1988 for the fourth Experimental Studio Series. Photograph courtesy of Jim Ouray.*

*Kurupira and Alligators from* **ANACONDA** *(1990).* From left: *David "Mufti" Matesi (Kurupira), Justin Kane, Laura Esping, Patrick Fitzgerald, and Julia Kirst as alligators. Puppet design by Dhann Polnau. Photograph courtesy of Salvatore Salerno.*

Hand-puppets from **LAKE STREET MAMBO** *(1990). Designed by Greg Carter, Greg Leirwood, Jim Ouray, Sandy Spieler, and Laurie Witzkowski. Theatre photograph by Warwick Faraday Green.*

*Eighty life casts were used in* **THREE CIRCLES OF 500** *(1992). Theatre photograph by Warwick Faraday Green.*

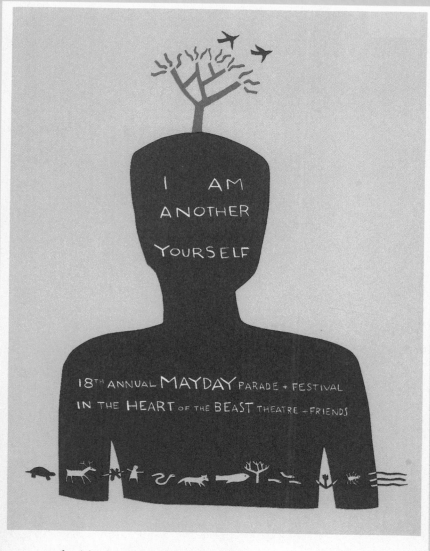

*"The Tree of Life! Gift for us
all!" The narrators shout as
the Tree of Life is raised in the
May Day ceremony each
year. Pictured here in 1991
with the theme "Return to
Turtle Island." Photograph
courtesy of Salvatore Salerno.*

*The Duke and Duchess from*
**DON QUIXOTE** *(1993). Puppet
design by Paul Chamberlain;
costume design by Margaret
Chamberlain. Photograph
courtesy of Jim Ouray.*

[OPPOSITE]

*Larry Trapp is haunted by
his former self as a Grand
Dragon in the Ku Klux Klan
in* **BEFRIENDED BY THE ENEMY**
*(1993). Puppet design by
Sandy Spieler. Photograph
courtesy of Greg Carter.*

*The Banker sings with his
dancing money bags in* **THIS
LAND** *(1993). Half-mask by
Paul Chamberlain. Worn
by Danny Schmitz. Theatre
photograph by Greg Carter.*

*Sun and Moon originally
made for* THE MIRACLE PLAY OF
OUR LADY OF GUADALUPE
*(1994). Puppet design by
Sandy Spieler. Theatre
photographs by Warwick
Faraday Green.*

*Phoebe asks her father why some beautiful flowers are considered weeds in* OUR PLACE *(1994). Puppet design by Beth Peterson. Photograph courtesy of Camille Gage.*

*Detail from huge parade puppet of the "Gorgeous Fever of Consciousness." Designed by Beth Peterson for May Day 1995. Photograph courtesy of Gayla Ellis.*

*Elisande (Laurie Witzkowski)
chops onions while the old
man with enormous wings
(Lou Pham) flies into the
distance. From* **THE VERY OLD
MAN WITH ENORMOUS WINGS**
*(1997). Theatre photograph
by Rebecca Richards.*

**SING!** *from May Day 1998,*
*puppet heads sculpted*
*by Alison Duddle, Sandy*
*Spieler, and Duane*
*Tougas. Papier-mâchéd by*
*Jim Koplin and numerous*
*workshop volunteers.*
*Theatre photograph by*
*Warwick Faraday Green.*

# 1973
# 1998

## 1973
### A BOAT, A BOOT, A BOOK, A BALL OF YARN

On the Fourth of July, David O'Fallon and Ray St. Louis stage a performance of large puppets in Powderhorn Park in Minneapolis. At the invitation of Eileen McCormack, participants from this event set up a work space in the basement of Walker Community Church, an important spiritual and cultural center for the south Minneapolis neighborhood. McCormack joins them in creating puppets and masks. They call themselves the Powderhorn Puppet Theatre, named after the neighborhood in which they live and work. The group creates its work collaboratively.

### FAT KITCHEN and
### INTERESTING TIMES [FALL]

A two-part show about poverty and greed, using fat suits, pie-faced masks, and several large puppet heads. Performed at the Firehouse Theater on the West Bank, Minneapolis.

*La Befana (Polly Harvat) meets the Three Kings (Ray St. Louis) in the first performance of La Befana in 1974. Puppet design by Ray St. Louis. Theatre photograph.*

# 1974

## JACK AND HIS COW, ROBIN HOOD AND HIS MERRY MEN AND WOMEN, SECRETS, THE COW AND THE BULLDOG, THE WORM WAGON [SPRING]

Small-puppet shows by Ray St. Louis performed in parks, schools, and community centers.

Powderhorn Puppet Theatre holds puppetry workshops in the basement of Walker Church.

## THE FISHERMAN AND HIS WIFE

Sandy Spieler joins the company. Ray St. Louis directs the four-person show, with single curtain and small puppets, based on the classic fairy tale. Performed at parks and community centers in summer and fall.

## THE GRASS WILL GROW AND THE RIVER FLOW [OCTOBER]

An epic pageant in three parts performed on the Walker Church stage. Title taken from famous phrase in U.S. treaties with Native leaders. Features large puppets of Earth, Water, Fire, Wind, and the Seasons. Its middle section presents a Faustian circus of humorous yet diabolical characters, ending with a resurrection of simple faith that the grass will grow and the river will flow, despite human destruction. These themes and the dramatic structure based on ancient rituals will become central to future productions.

## LA BEFANA [DECEMBER]

Based on the Italian folktale about the old witch who sets out around the world to search for the Holy Child only to find that holiness lives in the hearts of all people. Using multisized puppets, a four-person touring team takes the play to schools and community centers. Directed by Ray St. Louis.

*Please note that this is a partial history. Demonstrations, commissions, residencies, and community events were often not able to be listed here due to space considerations.*

# 1975

## FIRST MAY DAY PARADE AND FESTIVAL

On May 1, Powderhorn Puppet Theatre, the Almond Tree Household, The New American Movement, and the Street Artist's Guild produce the first May Day puppet festival. For the parade, one hundred participants carry banners and the large puppets from *The Grass Will Grow and the River Flow*, accompanied by the music of two accordions. In Powderhorn Park, they enact a simple maypole dance, make speeches about labor, and stage funny puppet acts. Coming just two weeks after the end of the Vietnam War, the parade becomes a celebration of community and new beginnings.

## THE DEAD WOMAN RISES

Fourth of July performance in Powderhorn Park. A poetic story about two sisters, one who dies and the other who searches for her. Directed by Ray St. Louis.

## FEAST OF FOOLS [SUMMER AND FALL]

An ironically comic, three-person mask show tours to parks and community centers. Directed by Ray St. Louis.

## MAGNIFICAT [OCTOBER]

Inspired by the biblical "Song of Mary," the story deals with the contorted plans of modern society that obscure the intrinsic wisdom available in the world. Performed as a series of wordless vignettes with large puppets at St. Stephen's School stage in Minneapolis. Directed by Ray St. Louis.

## LA BEFANA [SECOND PRODUCTION, DECEMBER]

Tours to parks and community centers.

# 1976

## THE VALENTINE'S DAY SHOW: THE HISTORY OF LOVE [FEBRUARY]

A humorous and somewhat coarse story about various kinds of love. Directed by Ray St. Louis. Staged with large puppets at the Mixed Blood Theater, Minneapolis.

## THE ROPE BANDIT [SPRING]

A one-man touring show created and performed by Steve Linsner.

## SECOND MAY DAY PARADE AND FESTIVAL

Theme is "Noah's Ark." Company builds many new animal puppets for this parade, all in pairs, of course. Small parade workshops held in several community locations.

*The first May Day puppet parade, 1975. Theatre photograph from Walker Community Church.*

*Abraham Lincoln weeps, the Women of the Dust continue to walk. From the **Buffalo Procession**, a somber memorial for the U.S. bicentennial, July 4, 1976. Puppet design by Sandy Spieler. Theatre photograph.*

## BUFFALO PROCESSION

A mournful but dignified procession with a herd of large Buffalo puppets, followed by the Women of the Dust. Performed at Powderhorn Park on the Fourth of July during the U.S. bicentennial as a reminder of the earlier life on this land. A large puppet of Abraham Lincoln weeps, serving as a reminder of the sacrifices upon which our nation was built. Also performed at Nicollet Island in downtown Minneapolis. Designed and directed by Sandy Spieler.

### THE STORY OF RUTH [JULY]
Based on the biblical story of Ruth and performed by Ray St. Louis.

Theatre teaches a puppet course for junior high summer school.

### THE BUFFALO STORY and FEEDING PROCESSION [AUGUST]
A story about the killing of the buffalo on the Great Plains. The Procession addresses issues of hunger and plenty. Staged in New Orleans, this trip inspires Sandy Spieler to work on river themes.

**BUFFALO PROCESSION** takes part in the Continental Walk for Disarmament and Social Justice in Washington, D.C. [OCTOBER].

### THE CHRISTMAS STORY [WINTER]
A version of the Nativity story with a political bent. Performed at Walker Church and as a touring show. Directed by Ray St. Louis.

## 1977

Sandy Spieler becomes artistic director of the theatre.

### THIRD MAY DAY PARADE AND FESTIVAL

Parade ordered roughly according to The Seasons. First May Day directed by Sandy Spieler, and the first to take the structure of distinct sections, each with its own musical sound driving its energy. Volunteers, including artists from other theatre companies, begin to play more central role in the performance. Entirely new pieces are created for the parade, including the purple-faced women masks and several large flower dragon puppets. A more deliberate ceremony takes place in Powderhorn Park with the raising of the maypole at the end. Orréa Mime Troupe and Street Circus organize the festival following the ceremony, with performances by musicians, singers, mimes, dancers, puppeteers, and other theatre groups.

### THE RED SHOW and THE WHITE SHOW

Performed on May Day. A lyrical show with solo voice, *The Red Show* is based on medieval texts about the capture of the unicorn. *The White Show* also performed at the Southern Theatre, Minneapolis, with a choir of twelve women singing a lament for Anna Mae Aquash, a Native woman warrior who had been brutally killed that year. Both directed by Sandy Spieler.

### THE PRAIRIE CIRCUS AND WILD WEST SHOW

Fourth of July show in Powderhorn Park, featuring a string of circus acts satirizing the high jinks and tragedies of midwestern history and folklore. Scenes include tap-dancing Chickens, a satirical Annie Oakley, and Buffalo and Star puppets who are destroyed by the building of the railroad. Also performed in October in Powderhorn Park gym and American Indian Center gym. Directed by Ray St. Louis.

Theatre teaches in several community centers in Minneapolis and St. Paul.

### THE CHRISTMAS STORY

[SECOND PRODUCTION, DECEMBER]
First big company show directed by Sandy Spieler with people from the Almond Tree Choir. A version of the Nativity story with a political bent. Also emphasizes the women who protect and manifest the everyday miracles of love. Children form part of the cast. Performed on the stages of Walker Church and Mixed Blood Theater and as a touring show.

## 1978

### PRAIRIE CIRCUS AND WILD WEST SHOW AND RESIDENCY

Brookings, South Dakota [JANUARY].
A revised version of the earlier production. Directed by Sandy Spieler.

Exhibit of puppets and masks in the Cultural Art Center in Brookings and at the Oscar Howe Center, Mitchell, South Dakota.

The theatre presents Bread and Puppet Theater's *Ave Maris Stella*, cosponsored by the Walker Art Center and Almond Tree Choir.

### SONG CYCLE [SPRING]

Toy theatre show tells the story of a woman's life accompanied by folk songs sung by a women's choir. Built and directed by Sandy Spieler.

*"Farah Faucet" poses with the Railroad Baron and the Railroad Builders during a rehearsal for the Prairie Circus and Wild West Show in Powderhorn Park, 1977. Puppet design by Ray St. Louis. Theatre photograph.*

## FOURTH MAY DAY PARADE AND FESTIVAL

Theme of "Changes," based on the red (labor) and the green (spring festival) roots of May Day, one signifying the change that people bring about with the labor of their hands and hearts and the other signifying the springtime changes in the natural world. At about this time, the Free Speech section is added to the parade, where any community group can march, following the puppet "story" sections. Powderhorn Puppet Theatre takes over the organizing of the festival performances following the ceremony in the park.

## IN THE BEGINNING,

based on an aboriginal creation myth, and

## THE DESCENT OF ISHTAR,

based on a Sumerian death story [SUMMER]
Created for Wisconsin NEWIST Educational Television. Designed and directed by Sandy Spieler; music by Jim McCreary.

Sandy Spieler is invited to work with Bread and Puppet Theater in Vermont on their annual Domestic Resurrection Circus. She returns to Vermont for two more summers.

## LA BEFANA [THIRD PRODUCTION, DECEMBER]

New version of the folktale, with sixteen performers. An expanded journey around the world, with Befana changing sizes from very small to very large puppets. Befana also fights off her own inner conflicts, symbolized by the weeping White Befana and the frantic Red Befana. Designed and directed by Sandy Spieler. Begins era of Robert Hughes's music for the production. Performed throughout the Twin Cities and several engagements in rural Minnesota.

## UKRAINIAN CHRISTMAS SHOW
[DECEMBER]

One-person show designed and performed by Steven Linsner, based on traditional folk theatre form called "vertep," featuring different layers of action with heaven, earth, and hell. Small tour in the Twin Cities

107

# 1979

### VALENTINE'S DAY SHOW—ANNOUNCEMENT OF NAME CHANGE [FEBRUARY]

As the theatre expands its scope from the specific Powderhorn neighborhood, the theatre changes its name to In the Heart of the Beast Puppet and Mask Theatre. The name change marks a point when the group begins to define itself as a guild of artists.

### FIFTH MAY DAY PARADE AND FESTIVAL

Theme is "Wake Up." Growing numbers of volunteers involved in creating puppets and marching in the parade. The large puppet the Tree of Life, raised at the end of the ceremony in Powderhorn Park, is created in this year. Children from the community make papier-mâché animals for its branches. In the course of this May Day ceremony, performers take fire across Powderhorn Lake to burn down an effigy of winter.

Joan Mickelson works for a few months as business manager.

### THEATRE MOVES TO THE GUSTAVUS ADOLPHUS BUILDING at 1628 East Lake Street,

Minneapolis, and hosts an exhibit of puppets and masks [JUNE].

### THE MONEY SHOW [SUMMER]

Based on the Inuit myth of Sedna, modernized as a comment on capitalism. Designed and directed by Steven Linsner. **THE EVER-WANTING.** Initiated by Sandy Spieler to comment on unbridled consumerism. Both summer shows tour briefly, but the abstract and complex themes play poorly for their ice-cream-social audiences.

### FROGGY WENT A COURTIN', GRANDMA WATCHES AMERICA, AND THE OLD WOMAN WHO SWALLOWED A FLY [SUMMER]

Small shows tour in various combinations throughout Twin Cities parks and to small-town festivals in Minnesota. Created and performed by the foursome of Margo McCreary, Curt Sloan, Steven Linsner, and Sandy Spieler.

### RIVER MUMMER RIVER [OCTOBER]

An odd dream cycle, performed with recorded music, featuring puppets from existing repertoire. Directed by Steven Linsner. Touring show to many locations in the Twin Cities.

### LA BEFANA [FOURTH PRODUCTION, DECEMBER]

Darker retelling of the Italian folktale, incorporating the character of "a robber of the heart of the world," who hypnotizes people into a kind of living death. Directed by Sandy Spieler; music direction by Robert Hughes. Performed at various sites in the Twin Cities and in rural Minnesota.

# 1980

Puppet exhibit at the Cultural Art Center in Brookings, South Dakota, accompanied by a residency at three Brookings elementary schools [FEBRUARY–MARCH].

### THE FIREBIRD [MARCH]

A one-person shadow puppet show based on several versions of the famous story. Built and performed by Steven Linsner. Performed in the theatre's storefront workspace.

### SIXTH MAY DAY PARADE AND FESTIVAL

Theme is "The Year of the Child," referring to the theme chosen that year by the United Nations.

Sandy Spieler and Curt Sloan attend the Survival Gathering in the Black Hills, South Dakota. Sandy builds a hand-puppet show against nuclear power with conference children.

### JOURNEYWOMEN TOUR: RECYCLED TALES [SUMMER]

Margo McCreary and Holly Schwartz create and tour a small show on their bicycles in rural Minnesota. Perform "Coyote and Eagle Find the Sun" and a fable about a paper company that moves into town and pollutes the river.

### THE HUNT [FIRST VERSION, DECEMBER]

Presents the Nativity story translated to the streets of an urban neighborhood, offering a biting commentary on the Reagan administration's policies. Directed by Sandy Spieler; music direction by Karen Lehman.

*In the Heart of the Beast storefront in the Gustavus Adolphus building, 1982. Photograph courtesy of John Franzen.*

# 1981

**RIVER ALLEGORY**, work in progress on what would become *Oh! River!* performed for the United Puppet Artists showcase at the Walker Art Center [WINTER].

**SARAH LAUGHED** [FEBRUARY]
A shadow-show collaboration with Sandy Spieler, dancer Alice Bloch, and lighting designer D.K., performed in D.K.'s studio in downtown Minneapolis and the Minneapolis Jewish Community Center. Based on the biblical story of Sarah.

**WATER, WHOSE CHOICE?**
[FEBRUARY]
Month-long residency in Brookings, South Dakota.

Workshops and lecture demonstrations held in various places throughout Minnesota.

**THE CIRCLE OF WATER** [MARCH]
Residency in Marshall, Minnesota. Words for the production written by poets Florence Dacey and Philip Dacey.

**HOUSE OF MEMORIES** [SPRING]
Based on the myth of Eros and Psyche. Designed and directed by Steven Linsner. Performed in the theatre's storefront space with eight performers.

**SEVENTH MAY DAY PARADE AND FESTIVAL**
Theme "In Honor of Change." Public workshops held in theatre space to build the parade.

*The Bird of Earth, first made for the 1981 St. Peter pageant* Let the Bird of Earth Fly, *attends numerous demonstrations for social justice, pictured here with the Central American Solidarity Committee at a demonstration in Minneapolis, circa 1984. Jim Ouray holds the center pole. Puppet design by Sandy Spieler. Theatre photograph.*

**HALLELUJAH**, Bread and Puppet Theater's street show, performed this summer at The Gathering and other outdoor festivals, using woodcut banners borrowed from Peter Schumann, Bread and Puppet's director.

**TURN OF THE CENTURY** [SUMMER]
A show about "inner and outer" democracy for The Gathering in St. Peter. Designed and directed by Steven Linsner.

**THE WAR FOR WATER**
[JULY–SEPTEMBER]
A touring show based on a story written by Sandy Spieler and children from residency in Brookings. Directed by Sandy Spieler.

Lucinda Anderson hired as company manager.

**OH! RIVER!** [FALL]
Performed in the theatre's storefront space. The metaphorical tale of two brothers and their differing viewpoints about the river. Directed by Sandy Spieler.

**LA BEFANA** [FIFTH PRODUCTION, DECEMBER]
Directed by Sandy Spieler. Music by Robert Hughes and John Franzen. A cast of six performs in the theatre's storefront and tours to rural Minnesota and South Dakota.

**SHOES OF INFANT LIGHT**
[DECEMBER]
First solstice piece. Performed in unheated third-floor auditorium of the Antiques Minnesota Building on Lake Street, using the existing architecture for the dramatic action. The puppet show revolves around the audience, which pauses at various stations to follow "Infant Light" as it dances first on "the Wheel of the Year," then in "the Days of King Herod," and, finally, reveals its magic in "the Belly of Fear." Music by John Franzen and Robert Hughes.

## LET THE BIRD OF EARTH FLY

[JULY–AUGUST]
Based on a poem by Meridel Le Sueur. Performance and parade created for The Gathering, a national theatre conference in St. Peter, Minnesota. The theatre works in residence during the summer, building four big puppets—Sky, Prairie, River, Woods—for four parades and a ceremony that inaugurates the conference.

## THE STORY OF ANNA MAE AQUASH [SUMMER]
A small tabletop show based on the story of a Native woman warrior who was brutally murdered and whose hands were cut off by the FBI and sent to Washington, D.C., for fingerprinting. Created by Sandy Spieler.

A Gardener and a Priest—users of the River. For flowers, for blessings, all are tied to the River, one hundred feet long, in the May Day parade, 1982. Puppet design by Sandy Spieler. Theatre photograph by Avis Mandel.

# 1982

## LET THE BIRD OF EARTH FLY
[JANUARY, ST. PAUL]

## OH! RIVER! and THE STORY OF ANNA MAE AQUASH
[JANUARY–FEBRUARY]

Performed at the Gustavus Adolphus space. Repeat performances of *Oh! River!* adding the tabletop show about the life of Native American activist Anna Mae Aquash.

## EIGHTH MAY DAY PARADE AND FESTIVAL

Theme is "Water." Parade features the progression of scenes inspired by Sandy Spieler's small book *Give Me Water!* which presents the cycle of water used for the nuclear energy industry. The River puppet comes across Powderhorn Lake on a raft for the ceremony in the park.

## NUCLEAR FREEZE DEMONSTRATION, NEW YORK CITY [JUNE]

Puppets of Sky, River, Prairie, and Woods join tens of thousands for this massive demonstration.

Numerous protests against antipersonnel weapons production at Honeywell in Minneapolis.

*Oh! River!* and *Let the Bird of Earth Fly* performed for the National Puppeteers of America conference in Atlanta, Georgia [JULY].

## ROUND ABOUT WATER TALE
[SUMMER]

A mini-circus based on the cycle of water used in the nuclear power industry, performed on tour in the Twin Cities and in North Carolina.

Major residency on water issues for Hopkins/Osseo Elementary School [FALL].

## LA BEFANA [SIXTH PRODUCTION, DECEMBER]

Directed by Sandy Spieler; music by Robert Hughes. Six-person tour in Minnesota and on the Walker Church stage. The audience swells.

# 1983

## A LIFE OF HOH

[JANUARY–FEBRUARY]

Story follows three siblings on their journeys in search for the water of life. Company-created with writers Loren Niemi and Florence Dacey. Design and direction by Sandy Spieler; musical direction by Robert Hughes.

## NINTH MAY DAY PARADE AND FESTIVAL

Theme of "Water" focuses on water as the basis of life and on the boundaryless responsibility to preserve and purify our water sources. Many more individuals and community groups attend parade workshops and march in the parade.

Company lives at farm in Alma, Wisconsin, building puppets and rehearsing for what becomes *The Circle of Water Circus* [MAY–JUNE].

*The Women Who Bend to the Water. Larger-than-life puppets from* **A Life of HOH.** *Puppet design by Sandy Spieler. Photograph courtesy of Bob Olsgard.*

## THE CIRCLE OF WATER CIRCUS

[SUMMER–FALL]

Huge production that travels from the upper Mississippi south to twenty-one towns and cities all the way to New Orleans. Features residencies, Big Ring Show, Side Shows, and Parades with a cast of twenty-five adults, five children, and two dogs. Coincides with the Mississippi River Revival festivals on the northern third of the river.

**LA BEFANA** [SEVENTH PRODUCTION, DECEMBER]
Directed by Sandy Spieler; music by Robert Hughes. Six-person tour in Minnesota and performances at Walker Church.

*The River puppet and the Birds from the River States ceremoniously enter St. Louis, Missouri, on a river barge under the St. Louis Gateway Arch, for* **The Circle of Water Circus.** *Puppet design by Sandy Spieler. Theatre photograph.*

# 1984

## TENTH MAY DAY PARADE AND FESTIVAL

Theme "In Honor of Time and the Change-Bringing of Our Hearts and Hands" honors teachers of life, art, and community. Parade images are developed from a brainstorming session with ten-year-olds.

## WALKING ART CENTER [MAY]

Residencies, parade, and performance for the opening of the educational wing of the Walker Art Center.

## WATER, WATER EVERYWHERE

[SUMMER]

Touring outdoor show on water issues, with audience participation.

## EARTH CIRCUS [SUMMER]

Pageant based on the wonders of the earth. Performed in the Twin Cities; St. Louis, Missouri; and Chattanooga, Tennessee.

## RESIDENCY IN LIMA, OHIO [JULY]

Extended residency to build a ceremonial opening for a cultural center for nine-county rural area.

Theatre moves to the Roberts Shoes building at the corner of Chicago Avenue and Lake Street, Minneapolis.

## DUSK TIL DAWN [FALL]

The hero's mythological journey through the night and through his own death, performed as a wordless dance with masks and puppets. Designed by Sandy Spieler; choreographed by Michael Engel; music by Joseph Tornebene. Sponsored by Studio X-2 Collaborative, a project of the Minnesota Independent Choreographer's Alliance.

## LA BEFANA [EIGHTH PRODUCTION, DECEMBER]

Directed by Sandy Spieler; music by Robert Hughes. Performed on basement stage at Hennepin Avenue United Methodist Church, Minneapolis.

## THE HUNT [SECOND VERSION, DECEMBER]

Created as touring show and performed in five Twin Cities churches as benefits for the sanctuary project for Central American refugees. Uses larger-than-life, flat, painted puppets. Designed and directed by Sandy Spieler; music direction by Rachel Nelson.

Residencies conducted at Hennepin Avenue United Methodist Church, Minneapolis, and Archdiocese of Minneapolis/St. Paul; Country Day School, New Orleans; Southeast Missouri Council on the Arts, Cape Girardeau, Missouri; and St. Louis Arts and Humanities Commission, St. Louis, Missouri.

# 1985

### FIRST EXPERIMENTAL STUDIO SERIES [JANUARY]

First performance in the Roberts Shoes space. Curated by Michael Sommers, the series presents puppet theatre experiments in form or content. Pieces by Michael Sommers, Jay McHale, Marie Olafsdotter, Marg Rozycki, and Esther Ouray.

### LIGHTNING [MARCH–APRIL]

A puppet and mask opera dealing with the splits between heaven and earth, men and women, body and mind. Designer/director Sandy Spieler; librettist Florence Dacey; composer and musical direction by John Franzen; choreography by Rob Esposito. Staged at the Southern Theatre, Minneapolis.

### ELEVENTH MAY DAY PARADE AND FESTIVAL

Theme "Our World Home" uses the rooms of the house as metaphors for other things, for example, the attic is ancestors and intellect; the dining room table is a political negotiating table.

### THE CIRCLE OF WATER CIRCUS [SUMMER]

Company performs in Sweden and Denmark for Scensommar Festival, an international theatre festival.

### BEOWULF [OCTOBER]

An exploration of heroism in a modern context, based on the story of Beowulf. Combined actors theatre and puppet theatre. Cocreated by Michael Sommers and Loren Niemi. Performed at Loring Playhouse, Minneapolis.

### WHERE THE WILD THINGS ARE [FALL]

A few Heart of the Beast puppeteers perform the puppets for the Minnesota Opera Company's performance in Minneapolis and on tour to New York City, Chicago, Kansas City, and Los Angeles.

Theatre sponsors a tour of Bread and Puppet Theater's production of *The Door* at the Sabathani Community Center, Minneapolis [FALL].

### LA BEFANA [NINTH PRODUCTION, DECEMBER]

Jeanni Calvit directs a new version of Befana, and Mari Olafsdotter designs; music by Robert Hughes. Performances at St. Anthony Main, Minneapolis.

Residencies conducted in the Twin Cities at Roosevelt High School, St. Paul Academy, Burnsville Elementary, Sanford Junior High, and West Bank Community Development Corporation; in Minnesota at Duluth Elementary; Rochester Young People's Center; Omegon Treatment Center, Hopkins; Winona CVB; and Fergus Falls Center for the Arts; and at Riverfest, La Crosse, Wisconsin; Kohler Art Center, Sheboygan, Wisconsin; New Orleans Public Schools Art in Education; Country Day School, New Orleans; and Burlington Arts Council, Iowa.

*The Tree (Jim Spieler), the Fish (Esther Ouray), the Monkey (Sandy Spieler), and the Mosquito (Maj Britt Syse) present the poisoned water to the audience for help in* Water, Water Everywhere *(1984). Puppet design by Sandy Spieler. Theatre photograph.*

# 1986

## SECOND EXPERIMENTAL STUDIO SERIES [JANUARY]

Pieces by Jim Spieler and Scott Vreeland, Michael Sommers, and Nicole Niemi; curated by Michael Sommers.

## THE NIGHTINGALE [FEBRUARY–MARCH]

An adult version of Hans Christian Andersen's famous tale. Cocreated by Sandy Spieler and Martha Boesing in collaboration with the company. Design by Sandy Spieler; written by Martha Boesing; music by Charles Bailey. Performed in Roberts Shoes space.

## RIO CARNIVAL [MARCH]

Jiving spectacle for the opening of a St. Paul festival.

## TWELFTH MAY DAY PARADE AND FESTIVAL

Theme of "Corn," based on Meridel Le Sueur's prose poem "The Origins of Corn." This theme initiates a series of shows exploring our agrarian roots and contemporary agricultural issues and land policies. Public workshops held in a series of storefronts on the corner of Bloomington Avenue and Lake Street, Minneapolis.

## IN OUR BACKYARD [SUMMER]

A wacky masked clown show about summertime. The trailer that holds the show opens into the theatre set. Four-person show with Michael Sommers, Jim Ouray, Sandy Spieler, and Wells Emerson. Directed by Michael Sommers.

## ODD, I SEE [SEPTEMBER–OCTOBER]

Four-person children's matinee performed at the Roberts Shoes space and then toured to Arizona in 1987. A child's adventure in the city with lots of visual humor. Created by Michael Sommers, George Sand, and Jim Spieler.

## SUZIE and THE STORY OF CORN

[FALL]

Touring show for schools based on agricultural issues and the current farm crisis. Designed and directed by Jim Ouray, with Mark John, Kitty Kuluver, and Barbara Cohen.

## THE HUNT

[REPRISE OF THE SECOND VERSION, DECEMBER]

Performed at the Howard Conn Fine Arts Center at Plymouth Congregational Church, Minneapolis. Accompanied by puppet exhibit of angels and dogs.

## IN THE CITY ARTS

Theatre launches three-year collaboration to provide ongoing theatre arts workshops for urban youth at several Twin Cities sites. Directed by John Mentzos.

Residencies conducted in the Twin Cities at Philips Neighborhood Improvement Council, St. Paul Public Schools, Anwatin Junior High, Andersen Open School, New Hope School, Lake Country School, Northwest Minneapolis Parade, Peter Hobart Elementary, Playwright's Center, Folwell Junior High, Bethune Elementary, and St. Paul Cathedral; at Crookston Environmental Council, Crookston, Minnesota; First Lutheran Church, Sioux Falls, South Dakota; and Country Day School, New Orleans.

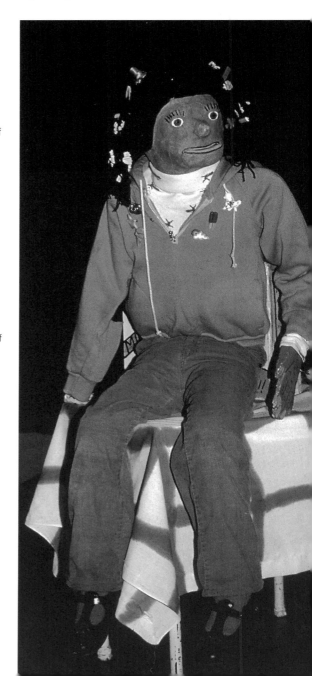

# 1987

### THIRD EXPERIMENTAL STUDIO SERIES [JANUARY]

A showcase of new image-based experimental work performed at the Roberts Shoes space, featuring work by Barbara Cohen, Jim Ouray, Heron Gardner, the Dreaming Crow Theatre, and more.

### TABLE, TABLE [WINTER]

Inspired by the farm crisis and the rash of suicides by farmers, this production also draws on "Origins of Corn" by Meridel Le Sueur in a wordless piece dealing with the economic policies affecting small farmers and the physical and spiritual sustenance of corn. Performed at the Roberts Shoes space with direction and design by Sandy Spieler; music by Steve Sandberg.

Big celebration commissioned by the Girl Scouts in honor of their seventy-fifth birthday. Directed by Nanci Olesen and Busara Whittaker and performed in the Hubert H. Humphrey Metrodome in Minneapolis.

### THIRTEENTH MAY DAY PARADE AND FESTIVAL

Theme is "We May Be Family After All," a quote by Chief Seattle from his famous 1854 speech about "our common destiny." Planned in response to the observance of the two-hundredth anniversary of the U.S. Constitution. Theatre uses the commemoration as a time to consider who we are as families—private, community, national, and human. Public workshops held in the Roberts Shoes space, which by now has expanded across half of the third floor.

Sandy Spieler on leave for a year. Jeani Calvit and Jim Ouray share artistic leadership in her absence.

### IN OUR BACKYARD [SUMMER]

Touring revival of 1986 show with a new cast. Directed by Jeani Calvit; performed by Jim Spieler, Sibban Ericson, Marg Rozycki, and Rhonda Lund.

### PRAYER FOR THE LIFE OF THE WORLD [SUMMER]

A pageant version of the biblical story of the prodigal son, commissioned for a national convention of liturgical musicians held in Minneapolis. Designed by Sandy Spieler; directed by Laurie Witzkowski.

**ELI** by Barbara Cohen and **ANACONDA** by the Dreaming Crow Theatre Collective [NOVEMBER].

Works in progress at Heart of the Beast studio.

### TIDINGS OF COMFORT AND JOY [DECEMBER]

A tabletop holiday show, designed and directed by Michael Sommers; performed by Esther Ouray and Megan Grundy.

Residencies in the Twin Cities at Chaska Elementary, Greater Minneapolis Area Girl Scouts, National Conference of Church Women, and St. Mary's Basilica; and at River Trails Girl Scout Council, Rochester, Minnesota; and Scottsdale Center for the Arts, Scottsdale, Arizona.

*Suzie sitting on her kitchen table from* **The Story of Corn** *(1986). Puppet design by Jim Ouray. Photograph courtesy of Jim Ouray.*

# 1988

## FOURTH EXPERIMENTAL STUDIO SERIES [JANUARY]

Features work by Jim Ouray, Steve Sandberg, Jim McCreary, Dhann Polnau, Sandy Spieler, Esther Ouray, Mina Wood, Kurt Hunter, Loren Niemi, and more.

## SUZIE AND THE AMAZING PLANET [SPRING]

A school touring show that explores the ecology of the earth as a whole, living organism through the adventures of a brave little girl. Directed and designed by Jim Ouray with Kitty Kuluvar, Mark John, and Barbara Cohen.

## FOURTEENTH MAY DAY PARADE AND FESTIVAL

Theme is "When the Dragon Speaks," taken from the words of many poets and dedicated to the spirit of people who are like the dandelion—brilliant and resilient.

Extended residency working with all ages in Ely and Tower, Minnesota [SUMMER].

## MOVE TO AVALON THEATER

at 1500 East Lake Street [SUMMER]
Built in 1937 as a moviehouse, the Avalon became a pornographic theater in the 1950s. In 1984, neighbors successfully organized to close it. The building was vacant until Heart of the Beast moved in.

Housewarming and blessing for the Avalon Theater [SEPTEMBER]. Celebration with cake, performances, and zany tours of the building.

## FIFTH EXPERIMENTAL STUDIO SERIES, HOUSE OF MYSTERIES [OCTOBER]

Labyrinth of performance installations based on the tradition of Halloween haunted houses. Works by Mina Wood, Liz Vessel, Jim Ouray, Loren Kellen, Dhann Polnau, Jeanna Lake, Sandy Spieler, Esther Ouray, Maj Britt-Syse, and Kurt Hunter. Masked ball held on Halloween night.

## LA BEFANA [TENTH PRODUCTION, DECEMBER]

Restaging and expanded cast as first main-stage show in the new theatre space. Directed by Sandy Spieler; music by Robert Hughes.

Residencies in the Twin Cities at Washington Elementary, Minneapolis Fine Arts Department, and Merriam Park Community; at Nett Lake Community Education and Bois Forte Head Start, Nett Lake, Minnesota; and at Metairie Park Country Day School, Country Day Creative Arts, New Orleans.

# 1989

## THE INVISIBLE CHILD [FEBRUARY]

Based on the story by Tove Jansson. Directed by Jeani Calvit. Designed by Mari Olafsdotter, featuring black-light puppet technique designed by Rostia Cerny from Czechoslovakia. Music composed and directed by Severin Behnen, featuring the vocal work of Petra Zilliacus.

## FIFTEENTH MAY DAY PARADE AND FESTIVAL

Theme "Voices of Trees" honors the generosity of trees and forests to humans, and of humans who grow like trees in their generosity. Also honors martyrs of the labor movement. Features 120 people carrying Norway pine seedlings (later planted throughout the community) led by Johnny Appleseed.

## SUZIE AND THE AMAZING PLANET [MAY]

Main-stage production in the Avalon Theater.

Wilma Wernick becomes managing director of the theatre [JUNE].

## A SONG FOR THE EARTH [SUMMER]

One-person touring show commissioned by the Land Stewardship Project to advance discussion of how agricultural land is valued. Created by Jim Ouray.

## THE REAPERS' TALE: A CELEBRATION IN THE HOUSE OF THE DEAD, FEATURING THE GRAND FEAST OF THE SKELETONS AND THEIR REENACTMENT OF THE GREAT VOYAGE OF CHRISTOPHER COLUMBUS IN HONOR OF THE LIFE OF THE WORLD [SEPTEMBER–NOVEMBER]

The first production in the quincentennial series. Entire production performed by skeletons, inspired by the Mexican festival of Day of the Dead. Cocreated by Laurie Witzkowski, Martha Boesing, and Sandy Spieler with the company; music by Robert Rumbolz. Local theatre critic Robert Collins calls the play "a phantasmagoric tale in which the dead rise up from the grave to spin a story of paradise destroyed by greed" (*Twin Cities Reader*, October 4–10, 1989).

## LA BEFANA [ELEVENTH PRODUCTION, DECEMBER]

Directed by Sandy Spieler. Music by Severin Behnen. Performed at the Avalon Theater.

Residency conducted at Blue Earth High School, Blue Earth, Minnesota.

Johnny Appleseed cradles the fragile sapling from the fifteenth May Day, "Voices of Trees." Puppet design by Greg Leierwood. Photograph courtesy of John Franzen.

## 1990

### SIXTH EXPERIMENTAL STUDIO SERIES, with LAKE STREET MAMBO [FEBRUARY–MARCH]

Based on soap-opera format with stories drawn from life along Lake Street. Hand-puppet show with four different episodes. Designed by Jim Ouray; written and performed by theatre's artistic staff: Greg Leierwood, Greg Carter, Mark John, Sandy Spieler, Laurie Witzkowski, Jim Ouray. Experimental series includes work by such artists as Anita White, Andy Wroble, John Devine, Margo McCreary, Beth Peterson, Ruth Hampton, David Korish, Holly Schwartz, among others; curated by Jim Ouray.

### SIXTEENTH MAY DAY PARADE AND FESTIVAL

Theme "Wheel of Change Everwhirling" applauds powerful process of change—particularly this year's dismantling of the Berlin Wall and the freeing of South African leader Nelson Mandela. Parade features a ten-foot-tall Wheel of Change that rolls in the parade, breaking through three constructed Walls that threaten to block the procession (Wall of Racism, Wall of Degradation to the Earth, and Wall of Commercialism).

Formation of CHIRP (Continental Historical Reclamation Project) to envision the theatre's quincentennial work [SUMMER].

Theatre begins a plan to purchase the Avalon Theater. The first steps toward ownership succeed when the theatre receives a short-term loan from the Minneapolis Community Development Agency. In August, the Minneapolis City Council approves the loan.

## ANACONDA [SEPTEMBER–OCTOBER]

A play about rain forests, celebrating the creatures who live there and warning of the destruction they face. Puppet design uses the bodies of puppeteers as a critical component, resulting in a sensuous movement style. One scene features a dance with live snakes. Directed and designed by Dhann Polnau, with additional puppets by Paul Chamberlain and musical direction by William Fehlow.

The theatre presents Brazilian puppeteers Masamente, with cosponsorship by Walker Art Center and Twin Cities Puppeteers.

## DISCOVER AMERICA

Second of the quincentennial productions. Created for school audiences, it focuses on the world of the Americas prior to the coming of Columbus. Directed by Laurie Witzkowski; written by Roy McBride, Lori Mollenhof, Beth Peterson, and Laurie Witzkowski; designed by Sandy Spieler with Greg Leierwood.

## THE INVISIBLE CHILD [DECEMBER]

Repeat of the 1989 performance.

Residencies conducted in the Twin Cities at Oak Park Elementary, Midway Coalition and Community Education, Hennepin Avenue United Methodist Church, and Andersen Open School; and in Minnesota at Spring Valley Elementary, Blooming Prairie Elementary, Ortonville Public Schools, Crookston Friends of MEEB, and Otter Lake Elementary.

*The Everwhirling Wheel of Change will burst through the three walls blocking the entire street on May Day 1990. Wheel designed by Jim Ouray, Mollie O'Conner, and Janet Hlebaen. Theatre photograph.*

# 1991

## SEVENTH EXPERIMENTAL STUDIO SERIES, TALES FROM THE AFTERMATH, 1492–1991
[FEBRUARY]

One of the quincentennial productions. Artists invited to create pieces on the legacy of the Conquistadors in America. Works created by Larry Cloud Morgan, Sandra Self and Fr. James Notebert, Greg Carter, Loren and Nicole Niemi, Jeani Calvit and Severin Behnen, Mila Llauger, Dong Il Lee, and Kohl Miner.

## CHÉ'S LOUNGE [FEBRUARY]

The first of the after-hours cabarets, occasionally running simultaneously with main-stage and experimental shows, serving great entertainment and food in the intimate setting of the Avalon lobby. Hosted by Roy McBride and Lucinda Anderson.

## ON THE DAY YOU WERE BORN
[MARCH]

Based on the famous children's picture book by Debra Frasier about the marvels of the natural and planetary worlds on the day of a child's birth. The Planetary Midway section, a series of booths with small puppet shows, celebrates the wonders of the world. The Narrative Story is told through three large set pieces that continue to transform to evoke the pages of the picture book. Conceived by Sandy Spieler, Esther Ouray, and Debra Frasier; designed by Debra Frasier and Sandy Spieler; Planetary Midway section designed by Debra Frasier and theatricalized by Laurie Witzkowski; built by John Synder; music by Sue Haas. In May, short tour to New York City and Canada.

## SEVENTEENTH MAY DAY PARADE AND FESTIVAL

Theme is "Return to Turtle Island," the Native name for North America. The parade honors "the deep roots of the great tree of peace" that was planted long ago by the Iroquois Confederacy. A highlight is the giant Turtle puppet with the Mother of All Nations planting the Tree of Peace on the Turtle's back.

Nadya Reubenova becomes executive director of the theatre.

## LAKE STREET THEATRE CLUB
[FIRST SUMMER]

Company members Beth Peterson and Roy McBride begin a free summer program for neighborhood youth. The theatre pays local teens to be interns, mentoring young children who take part. Using their own dreams and visions, the children work with artists to create puppets, masks, and performances that they then enact for parents, neighbors, and each other.

Ceremony and design commission for National Lutheran Youth gathering in Dallas, Texas [JULY].

## SEVEN DEADLY SINS OF LAKE STREET [OCTOBER]

Big Halloween extravaganza, designed and directed by Jim Ouray.

## STORIES FOR WINTER EARS
[FALL AND WINTER]

Commission by the Indian Health Board. Native American artists create a touring show based on Anishinaabe and Dakota stories. Featuring the work of Chris Warren, Rodney Banashley, Joni, Eva Two Crow with Sandy Spieler and Beth Peterson.

## THE INVISIBLE CHILD
[REVIVAL, NOVEMBER 1991–JANUARY 1992]

Directed by Jeani Calvit; music by Severin Behnen.

## LA BEFANA
[TWELFTH PRODUCTION, DECEMBER 1991–JANUARY 1992]

Directed by Sandy Spieler; music by Severin Behnen.

*The Mother of All Nations (designed by Eva Two Crow and Laurie Witzkowski) plants the Tree of Great Peace on the back of the Turtle (designed by Duane Tougas), May Day 1991, "Return to Turtle Island." Theatre photograph.*

Residencies conducted in the Twin Cities at Armstrong Elementary, Minnesota Association of Community, Como Elementary, and People of Phillips; and at Country Day Creative Arts, New Orleans.

*From a residency with Little Earth of United Tribes. Children preparing for a Phillips neighborhood parade, 1991. Teacher Jim Ouray. Theatre photograph.*

# 1992

## EIGHTEENTH MAY DAY PARADE AND FESTIVAL

Theme "I Am Another Yourself" counters the oppression of greed and racism. "In our ceremony this year, we honor the multitude of people coming together, neighbor with neighbor, sharing stories, building relationships and communities to walk forward along a path that diverges from the one laid down by the rule of greed. Be a LOVE WARRIOR. Say 'I am another yourself' to your neighbor, say it to the river, to the singing bird. The Tree of Life will flourish!" (Jim Ouray for the May Day tabloid).

## ON THE DAY YOU WERE BORN
[SPRING]
Midwest tour.

## BRIDGET OF THE FOUR FIRES
[JUNE]
Ceremony for the University of Minnesota art department's Women's Iron Pour.

## LAKE STREET THEATRE CLUB
[SECOND SUMMER]
Theme is "Circus of the Future."

## THREE CIRCLES OF 500 [OCTOBER]
The final piece in the series of works on the quincentennial. Performed at South High School, Minneapolis. A grand community pageant investigating three circles of five hundred years— the five hundred years prior to Columbus's arrival in the Americas, the five hundred years after his arrival, and five hundred years into the future. Envisioned by the CHIRP Committee (Continental Historical Reclamation Project); created by a core company of thirty people and performed by one hundred community participants; codirected by Dong Il Lee and Sandy Spieler; music by Carei Thomas and Severin Behnin.

Arts Plus begins. A three-year partnership with Ramsey International Fine Arts School, South High School, Heart of the Earth Survival School (all in Minneapolis), and Hopkins Elementary Schools. Directed by Roy McBride and Beth Peterson.

## SNAP THE TRANCE DANCE
[OCTOBER]
Halloween extravaganza performance, designed and directed Jim Ouray with music by Savage Aural Hotbed.

## DISCOVER AMERICA
[OCTOBER–NOVEMBER]
Midwest tour.

## BETWEEN THE WORLDS: SONGS OF LIGHT AND DARK [DECEMBER]
Winter solstice event, a journey through the longest night of the year, structured around a cycle of songs. Created with a core of nine women and performed by a chorus of forty women. Directed by Esther Ouray and Laurie Witzkowski.

Residencies conducted in the Twin Cities at Alice Smith Elementary, Eisenhower Elementary, Council of Performing Arts, Women Against Military Madness, Salvation Army, Beltrami Neighborhood Association, Elliot Park Neighborhood, City Parents United, Bell Museum of Natural History, and St. Paul Open School; in Minnesota at Jefferson Elementary, St. Cloud; St. Olaf College, Northfield; Council of Performing Arts for Children, Grand Rapids; Circle of Many Cultures, Bemidji; New York Mills Arts Retreat; Ironworld U.S.A., Chisholm; in Wisconsin at River Falls Middle School; Northeast Wisconsin Arts Council, Green Bay; and Lake Superior Elementary, Ashland; and at Country Day Creative Arts, Metairie, Louisiana.

# 1993

## THIS LAND [JANUARY–FEBRUARY]

A tribute to folk singer and labor activist Woody Guthrie and adapted from his writings, music, and drawings. Puppets are three-quarter life-size bunraku-inspired. Directed by Greg Carter; puppet design and music direction by Paul Chamberlain.

## EIGHTH EXPERIMENTAL STUDIO SERIES, PUPPET X [MARCH]

Featuring work by Galumph Theatre, Jeani Calvit, Katie Sjursten, Henry Hubben, and Margo McCreary.

## TARANTELLA [SPRING]

Feature film by Helen De Michiel, starring Mira Sorvino, explores a young woman's Italian-American identity after the death of her mother. Puppet sequences designed by Sandy Spieler.

## ON THE DAY YOU WERE BORN [SPRING]

National tour.

## NINETEENTH MAY DAY PARADE AND FESTIVAL

Theme "Let the Sleeper Awake" honors the rooster, which crows to "wake us up," inviting us to deeper levels of consciousness. The ceremony entreats people to wake up from the stupor of the rat race of life.

## LAKE STREET THEATRE CLUB [THIRD SUMMER]

Theme is "Around Our Block."

## DON QUIXOTE [SEPTEMBER–OCTOBER]

A version of the classic hero tale using heavy rod marionettes inspired by Sicilian folk puppetry. Directed by Jim Ouray; adapted by Jim Ouray and Henry Hubben; music direction by John Banks; puppet heads by Paul Chamberlain; costumes by Margaret Chamberlain.

First year for the South High School Partnership. As part of an ongoing class, South High students create puppets and participate in the May Day parade and ceremony. Beth Peterson, director; Sally French and Carolyn Light Bell, cooperating teachers.

## REIMAGINE [FALL]

Piece commissioned by ReImagining the Church conference, Minneapolis Convention Center.

## BEFRIENDED BY THE ENEMY [NOVEMBER–DECEMBER]

A true-life story of forgiveness by a Jewish family in Lincoln, Nebraska, and a man who was a Grand Dragon of the Ku Klux Klan. Style inspired by traditional bunraku theatre of Japan. Codirected by Esther Ouray and Sandy Spieler; designed by Sandy Spieler; musical direction by Robert Hughes.

Residencies conducted in the Twin Cities area at Jewish Community Center, Normandale Lutheran Church, Hopkins Public Schools, Windom School, National Lutheran Leadership Council, Valley Community Presbyterian Church, Minnesota Center for Arts Education, Wild Woman Artisans Guild, Bloomington Art in the Parks, People Serving People, ReImagining Conference, and Ramsey Fine Arts; and at Stonebridge Elementary and Stillwater First Presbyterian Church, Stillwater, Minnesota; University of Wisconsin, River Falls, Wisconsin; and Country Day Creative Arts, Metairie, Louisiana.

# 1994

## OUR PLACE [FEBRUARY–MARCH]

A sequel to *Discover America* about four ten-year-olds figuring out how to live with their families and with each other in their neighborhoods. Researched from interviews with local schoolchildren. Script by Roy McBride, Lori Mollenhof, Andrew Kim, and Laurie Witzkowski; directed by Laurie Witzkowski; design by Beth Peterson, Duane Tougas, Julie Kastigar, and Laurie Witzkowski; performed by Beth Peterson, Julie Kastigar, Andy Kim, and Elisha Whittington.

Prairie Island Earth Day Rally, Minnesota State Capitol, St. Paul [APRIL].

## TWENTIETH MAY DAY PARADE AND FESTIVAL

Theme "In Honor of Seeds: Awesome Vessels of Power" about the cycle of life and death, focusing on the need to protect and nourish our seeds and to celebrate their continual renewing power. The ceremony features the "planting" of twenty small children dressed as the Tree of Life.

*Performers are covered with mud and eating chocolate pudding for the MUD section of the twentieth May Day parade, "In Honor of Seeds: Awesome Vessels of Power." Design for the section by Alison Heimstead. Photograph courtesy of Gayla Ellis.*

### LAKE STREET THEATRE CLUB
[FOURTH SUMMER]

Theme is "Last Night I Had the Strangest Dream."

### SHIM CHONG [SUMMER]

A multimedia puppet show based on a classic Korean story of longing for a child, death, blindness, unrelenting love and devotion—and the miracles that occur on a young girl's journey. Created by Dong Il Lee, Beth Peterson, and Joo Yeo No. A project of Intermedia Arts and FORECAST Public Artworks.

Exhibit of puppets from *The Reapers' Tale* at the Lincoln Center for the Performing Arts in New York City as part of the Henson Festival of the Puppetry Arts [SUMMER].

### DAY OF THE DEAD— DÍA DE LOS MUERTOS [OCTOBER]

First annual procession of skeleton puppets to honor the dead in collaboration with Intermedia Arts and CreArte, a local organization of Latino artists.

### OUR PLACE [FALL]

Tours in Midwest and returns to the main-stage at the Avalon.

### BEFRIENDED BY THE ENEMY and DON QUIXOTE [SUMMER]

Performed at the Avalon for the Puppeteers of America regional festival in the Twin Cities.

### THE MIRACLE PLAY OF OUR LADY OF GUADALUPE [DECEMBER]

Styled after a giant retablo, a sculpture featuring saints from Mexican folk art, with masked performers and larger-than-life puppets. Designed by Sandy Spieler; words by Andrew Kim; Gustavus Adolphus Orchestra provided the music. Performed in the chapel at the College of Gustavus Adolphus in St. Peter, Minnesota, as part of its annual Christmas concert.

Residencies conducted in the Twin Cities area at South High School, Meadowbrook Elementary, Alice Smith Elementary, Kenwood Elementary, and Ramsey Fine Arts; and in Minnesota at Byron United Methodist Church; Mahtomedi Middle School; and St. Croix Catholic Church, Stillwater.

# 1995

## NINTH EXPERIMENTAL STUDIO SERIES, PUPPET CABARET [WINTER]
Work by Beth Peterson, Jim Ouray, Andrew Kim, Dhann Polnau, Anita White, Psychic Sluts, Julie Kastigar, Susan Hirschmugl, Paul Chamberlain, Theresa Linnahan, George Konniff; curated by Jim Ouray.

## LEAD RESISTER [WINTER]
Show commissioned by the Hennepin County Extension Agency to teach preschoolers how to prevent lead poisoning. Created by Beth Peterson with Bob Bannarn and Basil.

## TWENTY-FIRST MAY DAY PARADE AND FESTIVAL
Theme "Gorgeous Fever of Consciousness: Honor Your Senses" responds to the growing development of "virtual reality" experiences. Theme takes its language from Diane Ackerman, who wrote in her 1990 book *A Natural History of the Senses*, "To begin to understand the gorgeous fever that is consciousness, we must try to understand the senses—and what they teach us about the ravishing world we have the privilege to inhabit." The parade began with the imprisoning of Our Gorgeous Consciousness by the comically pathetic virtual reality world. Then each section went on to celebrate one of the senses, exploding finally with the colorful riot of the Gorgeous Fever of Consciousness. Bread served to everyone attending the ceremony.

## TREE OF 1,000 LEAVES [JUNE]
Ramsey International Fine Arts School residency and pageant with the entire student body of one thousand. Conducted by the entire art staff; organized by Roy McBride and Chris Griffith; directed by Sandy Spieler.

## LAKE STREET THEATRE CLUB [FIFTH SUMMER]
Theme is "The Great Hidden Mysteries."

Arts Partnership with Kelliher, Minnesota, with adults and school children in seven communities to create a giant school/community pageant.

The theatre presents the Mojiganga Arte Escenio, a puppet theatre from Mexico City, and Czechoslovak-American Marionette Theatre from New York City, both cosponsored by the Twin Cities Puppeteers.

## DAY OF THE DEAD— DÍA DE LOS MUERTOS [OCTOBER]
Second annual procession of skeleton puppets with Intermedia Arts and CreArte.

## OUR PLACE [FALL]
Regional tour and in-house run.

## LA BEFANA
[THIRTEENTH PRODUCTION, DECEMBER]
Directed by Sandy Spieler; musical direction by Robert Hughes.

Residencies conducted in the Twin Cities area at Alice Smith Elementary, Hill Montessori, Meadowbrook Elementary, South High School, Heart of the Earth School, Bel Air Elementary, Southwest High School, Sunnyside School, Ramsey Fine Arts, Kenwood Elementary, and Highland Park High School; in Minnesota at Wildwood School, Mahtomedi; Kelliher Public Schools; Cotton Elementary; and at Blaine School, Superior, Wisconsin; the Educational Theatre Association, Cincinnati, Ohio; and Weisser Park Elementary, Fort Wayne, Indiana.

# 1996

## SONG FOR A MILLENNIUM
[JANUARY]
Community collaboration thwarted by the breakdown of the theatre's boiler during the coldest January on record.

The theatre presents Eulenspiegel Puppet Company from Iowa City, cosponsored by the Twin Cities Puppeteers.

The theatre presents Arm of the Sea Theatre from the Hudson River valley in upstate New York, for a two-week run.

## TWENTY-SECOND MAY DAY PARADE AND FESTIVAL

Theme "Be a Bridge" is selected after public meeting discussions center on the violence in the neighborhoods and the need for stronger links between neighbors. Parade uses fences as symbols of fear, asking people to "de-fence" themselves by taking down fences and by taking a leap of faith to reach out to other neighbors and generations. Rose petals are strewn over the streets at the beginning of the parade by masked Connector Spirits as an act of faith against the violence that had grown so prevalent on these same streets.

*Lake Street Club for Teachers, 1996. From left: Dorothy Crabb, Luella Greene, Marilyn Cuneo, and Niama Richmond. This group went on to become the Women's International League for Peace and Freedom Arts Committee touring puppet troupe. Photograph courtesy of Ann Luce.*

## LAKE STREET THEATRE CLUB FOR TEACHERS BEGINS.
Focuses on helping teachers create their own puppet shows.

## LAKE STREET THEATRE CLUB
[SIXTH SUMMER] and **ART BUS**
This year the teens demand the time and space to create their own touring show. The neighborhood group People of Phillips provides a bus that the teens use as the Art Bus to tour their show. Its theme is "Heroes and Sheroes." The teen's show goes to summer schools, parks, community centers, and block clubs.

## BEFRIENDED BY THE ENEMY
[FALL]
Restaging of the 1993 show.

Kathee Foran becomes executive director of the theatre.

## BETWEEN THE WORLDS: SONGS OF LIGHT AND DARK
[DECEMBER]
Restaging of the winter solstice celebration from 1992.

Residencies conducted in the Twin Cities area at Pike Lake Elementary, South High School, Birchgrove Elementary, Crestview Elementary, St. Paul Academy, Park View Center School, Southwest High School, Frost Lake, Aquila Primary, Harding High School, and Johnson High School; and in Minnesota at Long Prairie School; Nay-Ah-Shing School, Onamia; St. Wenceslaus Elementary, New Prague; and Cotton Elementary.

*The Sun travels across Powderhorn Lake, May Day 1996. Photograph from video, courtesy of J C Bagdadi, Minneapolis Telecommunications Network.*

Futures
biggest gains
Commodities
Money market
yield rises from
5.01% to 5.03%
choice sends
stock soaring
World market
turmoil
investors'
sales, job figu

# 1997

## WEB SIGHT—THE TRUE AND AMAZING STORIES OF YOUNG HEROES AND SHEROES [WINTER]

Workshop production of stories about child labor and youth activists from around the world and around the corner. Directed by Laurie Witzkowski; music composition and direction by Elisha Whittington; designed by Beth Peterson; written by Laurie Witzkowski, Beth Peterson, and Andrew Kim.

## A VERY OLD MAN WITH ENORMOUS WINGS [WINTER]

Based on the story of Gabriel García Márquez. Using larger-than-life body puppets, the production has a haunting quality. Intermission features an interactive carnival with absurd freak shows with Old Man with Enormous Wings as the main attraction. Narration and music are somewhat improvisatory. Written and directed by Andrew Kim; designed by Sandy Spieler; narrated by Roy McBride; music by Scott Spencer.

The theatre presents Chinese hand-puppet master Yang Feng at the Avalon, cosponsored by Twin Cities Puppeteers [SPRING].

## THE STORY OF IQBAL MASHI [SPRING]

The true-life story of a young Pakistani boy who alerted the world to child labor conditions around the world. A fifteen-minute show performed for conferences, churches, and community gatherings in the Twin Cities. Created by Beth Peterson, Laurie Witzkowski, Masa Kawahara, Severin Behnen, and Elisha Whittington.

## TWENTY-THIRD MAY DAY PARADE AND FESTIVAL

Theme "May Abundant Blessings Flow" offers thanks for the blessings of our lives and a wishing for community wellness to counter the deification of the marketplace. The parade features a Ship of Hoarding, carrying King Midas, as a metaphor for the aspects of our culture that honor everything for its market value rather than for spiritual values.

## MINNESOTA RIVER VALLEY THEATRE CLUB FOR TEACHERS [SUMMER]

The company works with teachers from Montevideo, Minnesota, to create their own puppet show.

## LAKE STREET THEATRE CLUB [SEVENTH SUMMER]

Art Bus touring show with theme "Creation Nation Celebration Station."

## WEB SIGHT [FALL]

Main-stage production.

## THE SCHOOL OF THE AMERICAS [FALL]

Portrays the violence taught by this U.S. school for military training. Agit-prop theatre performed with larger-than-life puppets. Created by Duane Tougas with local members of Women Against Military Madness, Veterans for Peace, and St. Joan of Arc Church. Performed at various Twin Cities locations and at Fort Benning, Georgia; Washington, D.C.; and Ann Arbor, Michigan.

## THE HUNT

[DECEMBER]

Restaging of the Christmas story. Last produced in 1986, remounted because of the current violence in Chiapas, Mexico. Directed by Sandy Spieler; music direction by Rachel Nelson; featuring special guest singer Sylvia Maria Zuñiga from Mexico; performed at the Avalon and Latino churches in the Twin Cities.

The theatre retires its debt with the Minneapolis Community Development Agency two years ahead of schedule, becoming the official owners of the Avalon Theater on December 31, 1997.

Residencies conducted in the Twin Cities area at Schumann Elementary, North End School, School of Extended Learning, Edgerton Elementary, Brimhall School, Central Lutheran Church, South High School, and Powderhorn Community School; and in Minnesota at Orr Public School; Sebeka Public School; Nisswa Elementary; and Underwood/Battle Lake School, Underwood.

[OPPOSITE]

*King Herod (Laurie Witzkowski) prepares to send out his army for the slaughter of the Innocents in* The Hunt *(1997). Puppet design by Sandy Spieler. Photograph courtesy of Michal Daniel.*

# 1998

## TENTH EXPERIMENTAL STUDIO SERIES, EYE, EAR, HAND, MOUTH

[WINTER]

The roster reflects the explosion of new puppeteers in the Twin Cities. Curated by Duane Tougas; features work by Jim Ouray, Susan Hirschmugl, Matt Weathers, Sandy Spieler, Elisha Whittington, Anita White, Sam Ridenour, Suzy Deak, Margo McCreary, Shelly Chinander, Amy Ballestad, Willis Bowman, Mark Safford, Anna Stanley, Aaron Oster, Marg Rozycki, Alison Heimstead, Andrew Kim, Masa Kawahara, Elizabeth Garvey, Kate Brehm, Beth Peterson, and Alison Duddle.

Theatre presents Widiyanto Sariputra, an Indonesian shadow-puppet master accompanied by the Schubert Club's Gamelan Orchestra.

## TWENTY-FOURTH MAY DAY PARADE AND FESTIVAL

Theme of "Sing" celebrates the common beat of the universe and of life that gives us energy, that bids us rise to greet the new day and each other, and to SING! Parade features early earth songs represented by thunder, chirping frogs, stilt-walking ants, a huge frog float that is also a musical instrument, and enormous bats. Lift Every Voice and Sing features a walking, one-hundred-person choir and the "Harmony of the Spheres" with dancing heavenly bodies.

## LAKE STREET THEATRE CLUB AND ART BUS [EIGHTH SUMMER]

Theme is "Beautiful Wonderful Things That Grow."

Residencies conducted in the Twin Cities area at Highland Elementary, Castle Elementary, St. Mark's School, Southwest High School, Ramsey International Fine Arts, Kennedy High School, Falcon Heights Elementary, South High School, Arlington High School, Field Elementary, Clara Barton Open School, and Rainbow Families; and at Nisswa Elementary, Nisswa, Minnesota; and Principia College, Elsah, Illinois.

*Suitcase show designed and performed by Duane Tougas for the 1998 Experimental Studio Series. Theatre photograph by Warwick Faraday Green.*

# contributors

## MARTHA BOESING

is a playwright, director, designer, actress, and writer, and was a founder and artistic director of At the Foot of the Mountain, the longest-running professional women's theatre in the country, from 1974 to 1984. She has written over forty plays, which have been produced throughout the United States and in Europe. In addition to her collaborative work with In the Heart of the Beast, she has worked with the Minnesota Opera Company, the Illusion Theater (Minneapolis), The Actor's Theater (St. Paul), the Academy Theatre (Atlanta), A Traveling Jewish Theatre (San Francisco), and Northlight Theater (Chicago). Her work grew out of the 1960s, when she was a company member of the Firehouse Theater, and remains true to the political concerns of that time. She is currently touring her first solo performance, a series of monologues about the second wave of the women's liberation movement, *These Are My Sisters*.

## FLORENCE CHARD DACEY

is a poet, teacher of creative writing, and program assistant for the Southwest Minnesota Arts and Humanities Council. Collections of her work include *The Swoon* (Minnesota Writers Publishing House) and *The Necklace* (Midwest Villages and Voices). She has collaborated with In the Heart of the Beast Puppet and Mask Theatre on *A Life of HOH* and other projects, and she wrote the libretto for the opera *Lightning*, performed at the Southern Theatre in 1985. For the past thirty years, Dacey has lived in the small town of Cottonwood in southwest Minnesota, where she has been active in environmental, social justice, and community arts activities.

## DEBRA FRASIER

is an author, artist, and insightful philosopher. Her best-selling children's book *On the Day You Were Born* features her poetic words and paper-cut images. She worked with In the Heart of the Beast to transform that book into one of its main-stage productions in 1991.

## GEORGE LATSHAW

has been involved in puppet theatre for fifty years as a designer, actor, director, writer, and editor. He studied theatre at the University of North Carolina and at Yale Drama School. Since 1991 Latshaw has been artistic associate for the National Puppetry Conference at the Eugene O'Neill Theater Center in Waterford, Connecticut. He has been editor of *Puppetry Journal*, the publication of the Puppeteers of America, since 1983.

## ROY McBRIDE

is a poet, mixed-media artist, and organizer. He has worked with In the Heart of the Beast for over twenty years on the annual May Day Parade and Festival as a staff artist and as outreach director. He continues to be involved with the theatre's work in many capacities.

## DAVID O'FALLON

continues his work in the arts and in education. He still believes that theatre and the arts are powerful because they tell the truth, because they are the carriers of the image and word and hope needed to navigate these perilous times and to imagine our way. He served as the education director for the National Endowment for the Arts. He is currently the executive director of the Perpich Minnesota Center for Arts Education. He serves on the national steering committee for the Arts Education Partnership and on a research committee for Harvard Project Zero, and consults nationally and internationally on education and the arts.

## COLLEEN J. SHEEHY

is director of education at the Frederick R. Weisman Art Museum and curator (with Sandy Spieler) of *Theatre of Wonder*. She is also adjunct faculty in American studies at the University of Minnesota.

## SANDY SPIELER

is one of the founders of In the Heart of the Beast Puppet and Mask Theatre and has served as artistic director since 1977. She studied puppetry at Bread and Puppet Theater in Glover, Vermont, and Balinese masked dance at New York University. She is an accomplished sculptor, painter, graphic artist, director, designer, and performer of sound, word, and figure. Spieler directs the annual May Day Parade and Festival and other community pageants and celebrations as well as many main-stage shows. Sandy has received numerous grants, including a Bush Foundation Fellowship and a Minnesota State Arts Board Fellowship. During her tenure, In the Heart of the Beast has become nationally recognized as one of the top professional puppet and mask theatres in the country, having received, among other awards, the Twin Cities Mayors' Public Art Award and the UNIMA-USA Citation of Excellence in the Art of Puppetry Award, founded by Jim Henson.

# weisman art museum staff

**Lyndel King** ***Director***

Rose Blixt *Principal Accountant*

Karen Casanova *Public Affairs Director*

Karen Duncan *Registrar*

Rina Epelstein *Public Art on Campus Assistant*

Kathleen Fluegel *Director of Development*

Charisse Gendron *Development Assistant*

Pat Hefferan *Sales Manager, Museum Store*

Paige John *Senior Secretary*

Mary Kalish-Johnson *Curatorial Assistant*

Gülgün Kayim *Public Art on Campus Coordinator*

Mark Kramer *Exhibits Coordinator*

Bill Lampe *Building and Technical Operations*

John LeMoine *Operations Staff*

Patricia McDonnell *Curator*

Kay McGuire *Museum Store Manager*

Ann Milbradt *Education Assistant*

Laura Muessig *Assistant Registrar*

Jason Parker *Accounts Specialist*

Lance Potter *Events Coordinator*

Susan Rotilie *Coordinator of Youth Programs*

Colleen Sheehy *Director of Education*

John Sonderegger *Preparator*

Gwen Sutter *Associate Administrator*

Susan Weir *Curatorial Assistant*

Tim White *Preparator*

*In the Heart of the Beast Puppet and Mask Theatre would like to thank . . .*

Hundreds of coworkers are named in our memory and records for their
tangible work contributed over the years. The list is long, this space
is small. Here is the list of staff, board, workshop leaders, and directors
from the past twenty-five years in rough chronological order:

t h a n k   y o u

David O'Fallon
Ray St. Louis
Eileen McCormick
Ann O'Fallon
Ric Watson
Polly Harvat
Sandy Spieler
Martha Boesing
Jan DeNoble
Steven Linsner
Curt Sloan
John Franzen
Dan Newman
Kathy Jenkins
Robin Fox
Margo McCreary
Leslie Knox
Jim McCreary
Steve Sandberg
Robert Hughes
Shelly McCoy
Ken Eisenbraun
Holly Schwartz
Paula Phillips
Gail Irish
Michael Malone
Bill Copeland
Edith Gazzuolo
Joseph Gazzuolo
Susan Gust
Harvey Winje
Dave Nasby
David Swanson
Tom Williams
Joan Mickelson
Jim Ouray
Esther Ouray
Marg Rozycki
Loren Kellen
Steve Epp
Karen Esbjornson
Nanci Olesen
Lucinda Anderson
Florence Dacey
Laura Littleford
Connie Harris
Bill Fehlow
Kevin Miles
Mari Olafsdotter
Maj Brit Specktor
Doug Cain
Scott Vreeland and Sam

Lori Bergstrom and Elliot
Mark John
Susanna Ryan
Finn Ryan
Chana Ouray
Nick Wroblewski
Susan Haas
Michael Sommers
Kevin Kling
Loren Niemi
Jim Spieler
Jane Urban
Lynda Jackson
Carol Newman
Sibban Johnson
Greg Leierwood
Laurie Witzkowski
Rachel Nelson
David Johnson
Mick Labriola
Sally Howell Johnson
Matthew Spector
Cecilia Schiller
Dean Hawthorne
David Harris
Dhann Polnau
Wilma Wernick
John Mentzos
Kurt Hunter
Kitty Kuluvar
Barbara Cohen
Busara Whittaker
Jeani Calvit
Bruce Blacher
George Sand
Pauline Pfandler
Christine Rosholt
Beth Peterson
Rick Meier
Roy McBride
Sharon Rod
Betsy Sohn
Denise Mayotte
Monte Miller
Rosh Preuss
Vicki Rosholt
Winona Wilson
Bruce Leier
Julie Stoneberg
Judy Tilsen
David Emerson
Amy Crawford
Bill Scriven

Jim Koplin
Alison Heimstead
Severin Behnen
Nadya Ruebenova
Bill Snyder
Paul Guerra
John Schwartz
K. Ruby
Rosemary Williams
Robyn Tjernlund
George Hoffman
Diane Fisher
Diane Dau
George B. Meyer
Lisa Belfiori
Greg Carter
Paul Chamberlain
Robert Rumbolz
Rich Wilson
Alan Goudy
Carole Seny
Cindy Gentling
Lisette Schlosser
Duane Tougas
Kathee Foran
Molly Ross
Ellen Hinchcliff
Julie Kastigar
Heather Baum
Julian McFaul
Chris Griffith
Mila Llauger
Rose McGee
Anna Stanley
Andrew Kim
Dong Il Lee
Joo Yeo No
Eva Two Crow
Lori Mollenhof
Noel James
Chris Warren
Carei Thomas
Louis Alemayehu
Paula Horn
Salvador Patiño
Leo Lara
Gene Zemske
Jeremy Iggers
Anthony White
Roy Taylor
Camille Gage
Pablo
Frank La Roche
Karen Prince

Laura Burns-Levison
Jill Weese
Siddharth Gopinath
Rodney Banasheley
Maureen O'Brien
Thomás Fleisher
Graydon Kouri
Vernell Wilson
Wastewin Gonzales
Alexis Vaubel
Clifton Hubbard
Jane Shuttleworth
Dick Danaher
Willis Bowman
Susan Hirschmugl
Elisha Whittington
Nicole Stanton
Nell Hurley
Jennifer Gostovic
Mark Safford
Marsha May
Colleen Casey
Aerin Vanhala
Larry Siegel
Paul Halvorson
Nancy Hurd
Donn McCoy
Joan Vanhala
Mike Hoyt
Theresa Linnehan
George Konnof
Matt Weathers
Amy Ballestad
Shelly Chinander
Cat Francis
Robbie Herbst
Esther Osayande
Loretta Day
Lu Pham
Scott Spenser
Kari Kjome
Beth Holmes
Masa Kawahara
Allison Duddle
Aaron Oster
Paul Robinson
Mary Jane Mueller
Anne Ulseth
Leslie Wolfe
Arthur Anderson
Marty Winkler
Nicole Amaris
Sean Barton
Bart Buch
Nhia Lee
Jebediah Wilson

134